USING STORIES to SUPPORT LEARNING and DEVELOPMENT in EARLY CHILDHOOD

A PRACTICAL GUIDE

Helen Lumgair

With contributions from Kanella Boukouvala, Helen Garnett, Joanna Grace, Dr Valerie Lovegreen and Dr Jo Van Herwegen

Jessica Kingsley Publishers
London and Philadelphia

First published in Great Britain in 2021 by Jessica Kingsley Publishers
An Hachette Company

1

Copyright © Helen Lumgair 2021

Quotes from *The Boy Who Would Be a Helicopter: The Uses of Storytelling in the Classroom* by Vivian Gussin Paley, Cambridge, Mass.: Harvard University Press, Copyright © 1990 by the President and Fellows of Harvard College are reproduced with kind permission.

Front cover image source: Lorelyn Medina/Shutterstock.

A CIP catalogue record for this title is available from the British Library and the Library of Congress

ISBN 978 1 78592 487 3
eISBN 978 1 78450 876 0

Printed and bound in Great Britain by CPI Group

Jessica Kingsley Publishers' policy is to use papers that are natural, renewable and recyclable products and made from wood grown in sustainable forests. The logging and manufacturing processes are expected to conform to the environmental regulations of the country of origin.

Jessica Kingsley Publishers
Carmelite House
50 Victoria Embankment
London EC4Y 0DZ

www.jkp.com

To Jack
Where the story began

To Olive Rose
For all the stories yet to be told

Contents

Introduction

I was born and raised in a society where the majority of the population was disenfranchised, where many people's stories went untold, their voices silenced.

Apartheid South Africa was a place where those protesting the system were brutalized for their attempts to gain a sense of agency over their own lives and punished for their activism. The small number of individuals attempting to aid them in their struggle were also monitored and intimidated, with serious punishments at times administered as a result.

I often wonder if more equitable change would have come about, and sooner, had a larger percentage of the privileged minority listened to the stories of the majority of the people we lived among, enabling us to perceive their individual humanity and to empathize with them rather than accepting the distorted representation of groups as a whole, being made to fear that these others posed a threat to our very existence.

But, of course, this is often how leaders obtain, solidify and entrench their hold on power; this is the manner in which dictators rule and societies become oppressed, with certain groups marginalized. Populations are divided and told that others are other, narrative is weaponized and false narratives abound while *literature is censored and banned.*

Why? Because the stories of others compose the very threads of the universal fabric that connects us, allowing us to glimpse the humanity, the personhood of these so-called others.

I have a clear childhood memory of being in The Workshop mall in Durban, South Africa, at the age of 12. It was a Saturday afternoon, and I was shopping with my family, when an alarm went off signalling a possible bomb in the building. Mass panic ensued. There was chaos as people ran, looted and trampled each other. We managed to exit the building, and as it turned out, there was thankfully no device in the mall. A bomb blast had, however, occurred in a nearby Metro theatre (*New York Times* 1988), which was screening the film *Cry Freedom*, the story of the Black Consciousness leader and anti-apartheid activist Steve Biko (IMDB n.d.). The group claiming responsibility was the AWB (Afrikaner Weerstandsbeweging: meaning Afrikaner Resistance Movement, a South African neo-Nazi white supremacist and paramilitary organization) who were trying to disrupt the screening of Biko's life story. It would be years before I would see the film as an adult living in the United Kingdom, and it was only then that I came to understand the threat this biographical tale posed to those wishing to maintain the status quo, with its powerful depiction of a non-violent activist seeking equality and justice for all South Africans, and the unequivocal truth of his subsequent murder at the hands of those in power.

You see, stories illuminate. The light of story is beamed onto events and issues, infusing them with personhood, with emotional content and social meaning. Stories offer hope (a belief that things can be different) and solace (a balm for when they are not). They extend a sense of camaraderie: an understanding that what we are feeling has been felt by others, that we are not isolated and alone in our sorrow, our joy, and the spectrum of emotions besides.

Indeed, the stories of others are vital to our human experience. We need to hear about real heroes and fantastical superheroes, of people who have overcome brokenness and been made whole again. We need to be encouraged by stories that tell of underdogs taking on the powerful and winning against all odds, by those that portray triumph over disaster, tell of regaining that which was lost, and by those that speak of redemption, renewal, rebuilding and resurgence.

Stories can also, at times, present us with strategies that help in navigating life's issues, sometimes providing us with solutions to problems. Stories can fortify and solidify or challenge and confront beliefs, causing us to enquire, to question, to search, to seek. They galvanize us. It is very rare that we will have little or no reaction to a narrative, with powerful stories often moving us to personal and collective change. They are an abstract means through which we are introduced to others and begin to know ourselves more deeply.

And because of this power that story wields, it can be used as a force for good and evil. Narratives have been used over the centuries to reinforce negative stereotypes, to instil fear, to divide societies and to convince people to take up arms. But they have also been used to foster peace, to aid in healing, to restore relationships, to build communities and to deepen understanding among peoples.

History has shown the power of story time and again. There are instances that prove that the pen – or the verbal relaying of story – is indeed mightier than the sword, with nations like South Africa and Rwanda – which could possibly have slipped into anarchy with an overwhelming desire for vengeance – saved by the stories of victims and the accounts of perpetrators of injustice.

But what does this mean for children? Why is story of such importance? Jonathan Gottschall says that 'children the world over delight in stories and start shaping their pretend worlds as toddlers. Story is so central to the lives of young children that it comes close to defining their existence. What do little kids do? Mostly, they do story' (Gottschall 2013, p.7). The late educator Vivian Gussin Paley says that play 'is play, of course, but it is also story in action, just as storytelling is play put into narrative form' (Paley 1990, p.4). And children are motivated to do both constantly. Why so? I believe it is because through story the inner workings of self and of others are brought to light. And as children begin to craft their own stories and to make sense of the stories of others, they begin to gain autonomy over their life experiences, which leads to a greater sense of agency. It is this insight, self-governance and sense of control, together with a curious rather than judgmental mindset and a sense of compassion for all sentient beings, that will foster resilience. These processes begin with story. It is story that does this.

As Doris Lessing (2007) says:

The storyteller is deep inside every one of us. The story-maker is always with us. Let us suppose our world is ravaged by war, by the horrors that we all of us easily imagine. Let us suppose floods wash through our cities, the seas rise…the storyteller will be there, for it is our imaginations which shape us, keep us, create us – for good and for ill. It is our stories that will recreate us, when we are torn, hurt, even destroyed.

As we introduce the magical power of story into children's lives, they can begin to:

- encounter delight and wonder

- share in feelings, thoughts and ideas that are not their own

- reflect on their personal responses to different stories

- build their personal narrative through the stories they choose to express

- understand the issues of justice surrounding story in terms of access, representation and expression – that all children should be able to enter into worlds of story, that all children should be seen in story and that all stories are of equal importance

- and believe in the potential that story holds to move and change us as people.

If we are able to do this, we can rest in the knowledge that we have planted seeds of story: ones akin to mustard seeds, that possess the potential for exponential growth, along with a love of learning that promises to both propel and sustain them for a lifetime.

Chapter 1

Why Story?

I recently stumbled upon a story about Robert Desnos, who was an activist in the French Resistance during the Second World War. Jessica Senehi, in 'Constructive Storytelling: A Peace Process' (2002), writes about Desnos' arrest in 1944 by the Gestapo and his transportation to Buchenwald. Once there he was tortured and, refusing to give up the names of fellow resistance fighters, he was made to join the other prisoners in the camp who had been taken from their homes, stripped of their possessions and clothes, separated from their families and denied basic human rights.

One afternoon, Desnos and some of his fellow prisoners were crowded onto the bed of a truck by camp guards. Everyone seemed to know that they were being taken to their death. Traumatized and weakened by a lack of food, the prisoners were mostly silent as the guards avoided meeting their eyes.

After the prisoners had been offloaded at the place where they were to be killed, suddenly, and with enthusiasm, Desnos seized the hand of one of the group, a young woman, and stated that he would read her palm. With exuberance, he foretold a wonderful romance, children and a long life. The young woman laughed, and others began to put their hands forward. Desnos began to tell other fortunes filled with joy and promise. The prisoners became animated and began to speak of the romances, children and lives they hoped for. They laughed and cried.

On hearing these stories, one of the guards began to cry. The effect of these imagined lives was such that the guards could no longer deny the prisoners' humanity, and they were unable to proceed with the executions. They loaded the prisoners back on the truck and returned them unharmed for the time being, and some lives were saved.

This is an intensely moving account of the power of story. The guards in this instance were deeply moved by the untold story that each one of the prisoners was yet to live out, and they were in turn compelled to consider the individual humanity of each person and, indeed, to spare their lives.

'Why so?', we may ask ourselves. What is it that infuses story with the power to affect us on both an emotional and a cognitive level?

Firstly, stories appeal to us because we are social beings with a need for *connection*. Peter Gray, the eminent psychologist, says that:

Stories provide a simplified simulation world that helps us make sense of and learn to navigate our complex real world. The aspects of our real world that are usually most challenging, most crucial for us to understand, are social aspects. Knowing how to deal with evil as well as love, how to recognize others' desires and needs, how to behave towards others so as to retain their friendship, and how to earn the respect of the larger society are among the most important skills we all must develop for a satisfying life. Stories that we like, and that our children like, are about all that. They are not *explicitly* about how to navigate the social world, in the way that a lecture might be. Rather, they are *implicitly* about it, so listeners or readers have to construct the lessons for themselves, each in his or her own way. Constructed lessons are far more powerful than those that are imparted explicitly. (Gray 2014)

And as children seek for connection with others, we are able to provide them with stories that explore the social world and relationships in all their many forms.

Secondly, stories appeal to us because they provide us with *meaning*. Emily Esfahani Smith, in her book *The Power of Meaning – The True Route to Happiness* (2017), lists the four pillars of meaning as belonging, purpose, *storytelling* and transcendence. She discusses 'making sense of our experiences and who we are through narrative' (p.41) and stories offering people 'explanations for why the world is the way it is and why they are the way they are' (p.42).

We tend to think of stories providing meaning more so in terms of the listener. But it is not only the listener who is affected and changed by story; often the composing and telling of stories can be life altering for the creators. Esfahani Smith (2017) discusses George Dawes Green, the founder of The Moth, a non-profit organization whose mission is stated as promoting 'the art and craft of storytelling' while honouring and celebrating 'the diversity and commonality of human experience' (The Moth n.d.), with Dawes Green saying that he has 'seen that the process of crafting a story helps the storytellers connect the events of their lives in new ways, gaining insight into their experiences and learning lessons that had previously eluded them' (Esfahani Smith 2017, p.102). Mary Catherine Bateson describes us all as storytellers who are involved in acts of creation which are the composition of our lives, explaining that it is by taking the disparate pieces of our lives, and placing them together into a narrative, that we create a unified whole which allows us to understand our lives as coherent; and this coherence, psychologists say, is a key source of meaning (Bateson 2011, pp.104–113).

Thirdly, stories appeal to us because they furnish our minds with *hope*. Hope can sometimes be thought of as a somewhat dreamy emotion linked to wishful thinking when it has, in fact, been defined as 'a dynamic cognitive motivational system' (Kaufman 2011); unpacked, this simply means that hope is an active, thinking system that motivates us. Emotions follow thought – and not the other way around, as some of us might presume. Research has revealed that hope is related to divergent thinking (the ability to generate numerous ideas) as well as academic achievement (Day *et al.* 2010). This is essential knowledge to hold as we choose the stories we tell children. The writer Maria Popova (2015) says, 'The magic of humanity's most enduring books – the great works of literature and philosophy – lies in the simple fact that they are full of hope for the human spirit.' It is through story that we infuse children's learning with hope, building their creative and divergent thinking skills. By choosing stories steeped in hope – the overcoming of obstacles through courage, determination, persistence, thinking and strategizing – and by encouraging children to see their own lives in story terms, with them as author, we affirm a healthy sense of agency (the capacity to act independently and to make their own free choices), which indeed aids them in the realization of their goals.

Lastly, stories appeal because we are designed to *feel and think* in stories. Kendall Haven, in *Story Proof: The Science Behind the Startling Power of Story* (2007), looks at the child's appreciation of story. He cites Gopnik, Meltzoff and Kuhl (2007, p.54) who explain that babies arrive predisposed to focus on characters and their behaviour. At birth, babies can discriminate human faces and voices from other sights and sounds. In the first few months of life – many months before they develop language – babies learn to evaluate, observe, understand and emulate the details of human emotional behaviour. Haven (2007, p.27) discusses Bruner (1990, p.78), who believed that a young child is highly sensitive to understanding events through a story structure, considering 'goals, motives, and the actions taken for their achievement (for example, "all gone", "uh-oh"), and is able to extract meaning from the events and actions of others' (Haven 2007, p.35).

This sensitivity seemingly underpins children's ability to relate to the sequential and social aspects of story, and to feel and think in response to the emotions and actions of the characters when listening to stories.

Gopnik *et al.*'s 2007 research explores the brain's story-related development and describes how:

- at birth: babies exhibit an understanding of character traits – they know to link voices with faces and to study facial expressions and emotions

- by 1 year of age: they understand normally expected behaviour – they consider sequential actions, and can grasp goals and motives

- by 18 months: toddlers understand cause-and-effect sequencing, connections between events, desires, goals and conflict in the name of goal-pursuit

- by 2 years of age: toddlers understand 'trouble' as a deviation from expected or accepted behaviour, and exhibit empathy.

We see that through a basic understanding of character traits, the consideration of sequential actions, the linking of cause and effect and the awareness of goals and conflict in the pursuit of these goals, children have a natural propensity to think in story format.

Many families begin to tell children stories from birth with some beginning even earlier and relaying stories or reading to babies in utero. Haven (2007) cites Crossley (2000, p.11), who says, 'We are inculcated from an early age to seeing connections between events, people and the world in a certain way through the stories told in our families.'

Children then begin to learn to respond to story format and questions in their immediate environment, and to further lay down these story programmes. Johnson (1987, n.p.) says, 'From the beginning of our language acquisition, we must learn how to construct our own story fragments in response to our parents' questioning of our actions ("How did *that* happen?", "What have you done?", "Where are you going?").' After researching young children's responses, Johnson concluded, 'For children, to explain is to tell the right story, that is appropriate to the situation, one that has a chance of successfully answering the questions put to them.'

And as children grow, they not only hear stories and construct their own, but they begin to play in story. Gottschall (2013) says that

> children play at story by instinct. Put small children in a room together, and you will see the spontaneous creation of art. Like skilled improv performers, they will agree on a dramatic scenario and then act it out, frequently breaking character to adjust the scenario and trade performance notes...for children make-believe is as automatic and insuppressible as their dreams. Children pretend even when they don't have enough to eat, even when they live in squalor. And this play happens universally – in every culture, amongst every people, and seemingly always has. (p.23)

If we are indeed designed to think and feel in stories as is evident from research, and if story is a tool through which children make sense of the world, then our role as parents and practitioners is to focus on the quality of the stories we share with our children as well as the quantity, immersing them in story as often as possible by sharing anecdotes, telling jokes, reading and exploring narrative in all its many forms. Cox Gurdon in her book, *The Enchanted Hour* (2019), describes sharing stories with children as giving

> them what in truth is already theirs. The books and artwork of the world are...the inherited property of every child... Nursery rhymes, fairy tales, legends, poetry, paintings, sculptures, the great body of classic literature...all these things belong to the young and ignorant just as much as they do to the old and erudite. (p.148)

It is, indeed, our duty to share these precious resources with children, allowing them to take impressions and experiences and to play them out individually and collaboratively. Paley (1990) says, 'Amazingly, children are born knowing how to put every thought and feeling into story form. If they worry about being lost, they become parents who search; if angry, they find a hot hippopotamus to impose his will upon the world' (p.4). Pretend is where children operate, working through feelings and solving questions that arise as a result of everyday life. It is here, in pretence, that they are able to seriously grapple with issues. In fact, this pretence is the child's real and serious world where they actively and unrestrictedly examine ideas (p.5).

Throughout this book we will consider children's aptitude for, and mastery of, story. We will examine story as a valuable resource and develop an understanding of the ways in which it can be used on a practical level. We will consider story in terms of language development, cognition, play and social and emotional learning. We will explore story and how it relates to mathematical skills and other curriculum subjects. We will learn about sensory stories: what they are and how they can be used. And we will be presented with the effectiveness of stories as they are used in a therapeutic context in various ways.

If we are able to understand why story is essential to healthy development and provide children with a childhood that teems with the life of story in all its forms, they will in turn develop a sound sense of curiosity, a rich inner life, a sense of self-governance and social understanding. Through the sharing of narrative, we can also impart the awareness that – at any given time – they can access or create a story, unlocking its many wonders.

NARRATIVE IDENTITY

None of us are to be found in sets of tasks or lists of attributes: we can only be known in the unfolding of our unique stories within the context of everyday events.

Vivian Gussin Paley (1990, p.xii)

Narrative identity is built as we compose and adapt our life stories based on:

- our natural predisposition to the structure of story as discussed above

- the combination of our internal and external experiences – our sensory experiences of the world around us combined with our inner thoughts and feelings

- the stories of those we encounter through our connection to them, and our relationships.

The late neurologist Oliver Sacks (1998) explains:

> We have, each of us, a life-story, an inner narrative – whose continuity, whose sense, *is* our lives. It might be said that each of us constructs and lives, a 'narrative', and that this narrative *is* us, our identities.
>
> If we wish to know about a man, we ask 'what is his story – his real, inmost story?' – for each of us *is* a biography, a story. Each of us *is* a singular narrative, which is constructed, continually, unconsciously, by, through and in us – through our perceptions, our feelings, our thoughts, our actions; and, not least, our discourse, our spoken narrations. Biologically, physiologically, we are not so different from each other; historically, as narratives – we are each of us unique. (p.111)

The concept of narrative identity can be described as 'a person's internalized and evolving life story, integrating the reconstructed past and imagined future to provide life with some degree of unity and purpose' (McAdams and McLean 2013). This story is created through the making of what is termed 'narrative choices', which is a focus on the most extraordinary events of our lives, those experiences that 'we need to make sense of, the ones that shape us' (p.235). 'Life stories do not simply *reflect* personality. They *are* personality, or more accurately, they are important *parts of* personality, along with other parts, like dispositional traits, goals, and values' (McAdams and Manczak 2015). Beck (2015) explains further that a person's life story is not merely about the events and the factual details of their life but rather about the way a person puts the events and facts together in order to make meaning from it. It is this narrative that becomes a form of identity where:

> the things someone chooses to include in the story, and the way she tells it, can both reflect and shape who she is. A life story doesn't just

say what happened, it says why it was important, what it means for who the person is, for who they'll become, and for what happens next. (Beck 2015)

According to McLean, Pasupathi and Pals (2007), a narrative identity is constructed over time as people tell stories about their experiences to others. Indeed it is the storytelling that fosters the further linking of experiences to the self. McAdams and McLean (2013) discuss the development of narrative identity with regard to children in more detail, citing research that has 'repeatedly shown that conversations with parents about personal events are critical to the development of narrative skills in children' (p.235). The research also showed that parents who themselves use an 'elaborated conversational style' (p.235) which underscores emotional evaluations of past events, and focuses on causes and explanations, tend to 'stimulate the development of strong self-storytelling skills in their children' (p.235) who then tend to demonstrate a greater degree of elaboration (p.236). They report that this increased parental elaboration is also associated with a variety of positive cognitive and socio-emotional outcomes.

The work of Reese, Jack and White, cited by McAdams and McLean (2013, p.236), also shows that 'early parent–child conversations provide the foundations for children to learn how to make meaning out of personal events' and, as we have learned, that 'meaning making… is a process central to the development of narrative identity'. The conversations we have with children where we recount their experiences together, and enter into thinking about them together, enables children not only to technically structure their lived experiences into coherent stories but also to extract meaning from them.

Indeed, literature about the personal narratives of children would indicate that the narratives are crucial in terms of several developmental processes including:

- the building of autobiographical memories

- the joining with others in a specific social-cultural context

- the ability to organize emotions

- the faculty of self-awareness

- the ability to 'view interpersonal situations from multiple pers-pectives' and the understanding that the self has various 'narrative voices' or sides.

(Adapted from Smith, Cowie and Blades 2003, p.358)

Additionally, Oppenheim and Warren (1997, p.289) find 'clear asso-ciations between children's co-constructed narratives with their mothers...and their behavioral and emotional regulation in every-day life'.

By having story-based conversations with young children, where we allow them to express their stories freely and to think about them further with us, we can help them to build healthy, self-aware and emotionally balanced narratives that focus on connection, belonging, identity and meaning. Anne Burke says that we are better equipped to truly listen to children and their sharing of 'pivotal moments' if we are able to recognize that their 'understanding of the world is enhanced when it is mapped as a personal narrative'. It is through their storytelling that 'children can be recognized as experts and agents in their own lives' (Burke 2012, pp.11–12). What is therefore imperative, then, is that in and through our story expression we provide children with the language they need to express themselves accurately in terms of their thoughts and emotions. Cox Gurdon (2019, p.95) explains:

Language allows children to occupy the world, their castle, as owners. It means they can understand and describe things with texture and precision. It means that if a girl sees a dog or a squirrel, say, moving with great speed, she can describe what's happening: is the creature darting or sprinting, racing or feinting, ambling or scampering? When something frightening happens, she can fine-tune her explanation: it was chilling, alarming, macabre, ghastly, daunting, or perhaps just unpleasant. *Gradations of meaning matter, because they bring us closer to the truth.* (Emphasis mine)

As children are given the freedom to find their own voice, the accurate language necessary to express themselves clearly and the opportunity to begin to create their own narratives, they can, in turn, reflect on the rich stories of others,

- identifying with them (or indeed choosing not to) through comparing and contrasting their personal stories, feelings, ideas and values with the ones presented to them

- gaining insight into the struggles and victories of others (real and imagined) as well as their own

- expanding their feeling and thinking through the assimilation of novel information

- further re-creating, modifying and refining their own stories in response.

Jean Paul Sartre (1964, p.39) explains, 'A man is always a teller of stories. He lives surrounded by his own stories and those of other people. He sees everything that happens to him in terms of stories.' But stories, life stories included, can be positive or negative.

McAdams, after working with life stories and meaning for 30 years and analysing hundreds of them, found interesting patterns in 'how people living meaningful lives understand and interpret their experiences' (in Esfahani Smith 2017, p.108). He found that people motivated to contribute to society and future generations were more likely to tell redemptive stories about their lives, that is, stories that move from bad to good, stories that extract meaning from suffering. In contrast, others told what McAdams described as contamination stories, where people interpreted their lives in terms of bad events overshadowing the good. In his findings, the people who told contamination stories were more likely to feel that their lives were less coherent than those who focused on redemption stories.

We see redemption as a theme in many picture books and stories. We are, more often than not, witness to resolution, to peace-making, to change, growth and learning on the part of the characters. Is there adversity? Often. Evil to be faced? Sometimes. Injustice, suffering, struggle and sorrow to grapple with? Almost certainly. We can therefore acknowledge emotions and affirm feelings and thoughts that arise as we tell and read, taking comfort in the knowledge that because children are designed to think and feel in stories, they are able to explore these complex ideas and to begin to make sense of them. We can be confident in sharing all of the aspects of stories together – including the difficult and uncomfortable ones – as they are, after all, a part of our individual and collective stories, and of life itself. And we have golden opportunities to continually model redemption for children throughout their childhood by continually focusing on the connection, making the meaning and extracting the hope from the stories we share. It is these elements that are the elements of salvation. And it is this focus that will work to instil a sense of agency in the lives of the children.

Chapter 2

Story

A Whole-Body Process

In the previous chapter we explored why it is that story appeals to human beings, and we discussed narrative identity, concluding that people are designed both to respond to story and to construct their thinking in a narrative format.

In this chapter we will explore story as a dynamic whole-body process examining what happens in the brain, on a cognitive level, and on an emotional (affective) level. We will consider the ways in which we tell stories, looking at effective tools for bringing stories to life.

THE DYNAMIC NATURE OF STORY

I would propose that the effectiveness of story lies in the way it functions as a personalised process. A single story can be made new each time a listener hears it, with one story told to thirty different people becoming, in essence, thirty different stories. Haven discusses Applebee (1977) and Holland (1975), who 'both showed that each reader creates a unique reconstruction of the material that the text provided based on that person's internal story scripts' (Haven 2007, p.30).

'How so?', you may wonder? When a listener hears a story, they bring to it their current emotional state, their experience and their current ideas and beliefs. The story is filtered through these lenses, and is therefore changed, with a new version created. Each person's understanding of the story will be unique, their perspective individual and they will extract from it a different essence. If a story is indeed made new each time the listener hears it, it can be considered to be constantly moving and evolving, and thus a dynamic process.

Many people's traditional image of story time is one where children are seated silently in a group focused on a teacher, or tucked up in bed, quietly listening as a text is read to them. Indeed, story is often used to quiet and to calm children, which it can, of course, do. But if we view it only in this manner, and not as a fluid, reciprocal process that engages both parties then we will have missed its potential to reach children at the deepest level. Story moves the listener: it has the power to excite, antagonize, anguish, stir, anger, bore, sadden and motivate. It almost always elicits some response. And therefore story time is not only about caregivers telling stories to children; it is equally about the children's responses: their linking of existing knowledge to the story being shared, their offering up of thoughts and ideas, their expression of emotions and their regaling of stories that are stirred in response to the one being offered to them.

The dynamism of story is also evident in terms of the opportunity it provides for children to learn about the external world, to connect this discovery with their internal world and to navigate these two worlds in tandem. Robinson and Aronica (2015, p.119) describe it thus:

> Children are not born into one world: they are born into two. There is the world around them: the world of other people and things that exist... There is also the world within them: the internal world of their own consciousness, which came into being when they did and exists only because they do. As human beings, we know the outer world only through our inner worlds. We perceive it through our physical senses, and we conceive it through the ideas, feelings, and values that constitute our worldview. If education is to fulfil the principles of a liberal democracy, it has to help children understand both of these worlds and how deeply they affect each other.

Storytelling allows children to access a variety of external world experiences and to evaluate them through feeling and thinking. It fuels the awareness of and engagement between these two worlds. Through one's own unique responses to different stories feelings are born and examined, and thoughts reflected upon. Gray (2014), quoting the work of Fritz Breithaupt, says that these processes often do not happen in real life due to a combination of stress, the defensiveness of ego or a drive to action, whereas 'in fiction, where we cannot alter what happens, what "we can do is feel, reflect, and think"'. This reflection extends to reflecting on the responses of others. As stories are shared, children are exposed to the differing responses of others to the same material, and the dynamism of story can further be seen in its ability to foster connection and understanding. The author Brené Brown (2015) says that 'storytelling and creating can be spiritual practices, because they cultivate awareness' (p.11). And the process of engaging in and with story is not only a mental, emotional and spiritual exercise but as mentioned above, it can be understood as a whole-body process, involving our physical capacities as well.

Paul J. Zak, Director of the Center for Neuroeconomics Studies at Claremont Graduate University, carried out research exploring people's responses to story as well as how highly engaging stories are created. Zak and his team (2013) discovered two key aspects in the creation of effective stories: first, that they capture and hold attention and, second, that they transport the story receivers into the worlds of the characters. Zak notes that the maintenance of attention in a story leads to arousal in the brain, an increase in heart rate and breathing speed and the release of stress hormones. And once a person's attention has been focused long enough, they begin to emotionally resonate with the characters in the story and, according to narratologists, are 'transported': that is they begin to feel what the characters in the story feel. This 'transportation', as Zak describes it, causes people to imagine the lives of others, helps to develop compassion for others and changes perspective. It is this transportation that promotes empathy.

Empathy is defined as 'the action of understanding, being aware of, being sensitive to, and vicariously experiencing the feelings, thoughts, and experience of another' (Merriam-Webster 2019). It is made up of two parts: affective and cognitive empathy. The affective part is the emotional response to emotions and emotional situations. The cognitive part is what enables a person to understand different perspectives. 'Emotion and cognition play complementary roles in the feeling of empathy. In order to feel empathy, you must experience another's suffering. But you must also know what happened to the victim – a cognitive process – in order to identify with him' (Feuerstein and Lewin-Benham 2012, p.121). Story encompasses both of these areas, providing us with opportunities to identify and grapple with the emotions of the characters, and to make sense of the thoughts, choices and actions of the characters as a plot unfolds.

And as these two areas are combined – emotion and cognition – it leads the children to make connections, examining:

- Causation: What caused the event/s?

- Values: Was the event fair? Why? Did anyone benefit from it? If yes, how so? If not, why? Was anyone hurt by it? If so, how?

- Reality: Have you ever experienced something similar? What were your feelings as a result?

(Feuerstein and Lewin-Benham 2012, p.121)

Gray (2014) says that a

> series of studies showed that people who have read a great deal of fiction – especially fiction of the type that deals with interpersonal relationships – score higher on various measures of empathy than do otherwise similar people whose reading centers more on nonfiction… In an experiment conducted in a low-income area of Toronto, the capacity of 4-year-olds to take another person's perspective and reason from that perspective increased greatly as a result of an intervention in which they heard many stories read to them by parents, teachers, and research assistants.

Engel (2016) says that 'story performs both inner psychological functions as well as social functions'. Michelle Borba in her book *UnSelfie – Why Empathetic Kids Succeed in Our All-About-Me World* (2016) says that reading makes us 'kinder' as well as 'smarter' and notes that although the current educational focus in the United States (on Common Core standards) is activating a move away from fiction to non-fiction reading in order to improve students' writing abilities, it is literary fiction that nurtures empathy and perspective taking. She also explains that 'picture books are richer in emotion-charged content than chapter books are, and it's this emotionally charged content (particularly in the first several years of life) that's crucial to empathy development' (2016, p.77).

When we read children stories about noble characters and noble acts, about courage and kindness, they are changed. Daniel Goleman says that usually when people witness acts of kindness, they are stirred to perform one too. The vivid telling of a story where kindness is central, psychologists believe, has the same 'emotional impact as seeing the act itself', and these social benefits of story may be one of the reasons that 'mythic tales worldwide are rife with figures who save others through their courageous deeds' (Goleman 2006, p.53).

But not only do we feel what characters feel and think about what they think, we also do what they do as our brains mirror their actions. Borba discusses a study where neuroscientists at Washington University in St. Louis watched brain scans from functional magnetic resonance imaging (fMRI)

> of volunteers as they read from selected material... If in the passage the character was 'pulling on a light cord', the region of the brain associated with controlling grasping motions would activate. If they read that the character had changed location...the region responsible for spatial abilities would light up. (p.80)

In a study carried out by White *et al.* (2016), 180 4- and 6-year-olds were tested through the administration of a boring computer task which they were asked to attend to for 10 minutes. The children had the option of quitting the task at any point and were told that if they became too bored, they could instead choose to play a game on an iPad which was located in a nearby testing room. They were assigned to one of three different conditions: (1) a control group in which they were asked to think about their thoughts and feelings as they went through the task, asking themselves, 'Am I working hard?' (2) a group in which they were asked to think of themselves in the third person (for example if a child's name was John, asking themselves 'Is John working hard?') and (3) a group in which they were asked to think about someone else known to be really good at working hard. In this instance they could choose from some recognizable superhero types: Batman, Bob the Builder, Rapunzel and Dora the Explorer. The children in this group also had the opportunity to dress as the character they picked. For 10 minutes, the children were able to move between the task and the iPad and were reminded through a loudspeaker of their chosen condition every minute; that is, they would be asked a question, for example 'Is Batman working hard?' All of the children were reminded of the importance of the activity and told that it would be helpful if they could work on it as long as they were able to. Perseverance was measured as the amount of time spent on the task. The results showed that the children pretending to be superheroes spent more time working on the task than those who thought of themselves in the third person, and both of these groups performed better than the children who thought of themselves as simply 'me'. The authors of the study, titled 'The "Batman effect": Improving Perseverance in Young Children', stated that 'Children who were asked to reflect on the task as if they were another person were less likely to indulge in immediate gratification and more likely to work toward a relatively long-term goal.'

Some further possible conclusions drawn from the study were of interest. Firstly, that pretending to be another person allowed the greatest separation from the temptation and therefore led to greater focus. And secondly, that when the children dressed up as a character, they identified with the traits of that particular character and wished to emulate them. This substantiates Goleman's statement about heroic acts stirring impulses in listeners who are moved to imitate them. Story allows children to self-distance, as well as to play out a character role by donning the character's clothes and carrying out what they feel would be his/her/its actions. In this instance, it led to positive, prosocial behaviours.

Another study which I feel is also relevant here is one carried out with adults and described by Paul J. Zak in the *Harvard Business Review* (2014), which explains how his laboratory wondered if they could 'hack' people's oxytocin systems in order to motivate them to engage in co-operative behaviours. The objective was to test if the brains of participants would make oxytocin in response to narratives shot on video. They took blood from participants before the viewing of the narrative and afterwards, and their findings indicated 'that character-driven stories do consistently cause oxytocin synthesis. Further, the amount of oxytocin released by the brain predicted how much people were willing to help others; for example, donating money to a charity associated with the narrative.'

From these studies, it is evident that story moves us in a holistic way as we are engaged and transported. It inspires us and it has the potential to change us: how we feel, what we think, what we do and, in turn, who we are.

STORY AND EMOTIONS

On an emotional level, story further causes us to:

- *Identify with a number of different characters, experiencing* 'vicariously the sorrows, joys, triumphs, defeats, and ethical conflicts of the protagonist – and maybe those of the antagonist, too' (Gray 2014).

- *Develop emotional literacy skills*: the recognition and expression of emotions and emotional themes and ideas. This can be done by ensuring that we are looking at the pictures together, noticing and then discussing the facial expressions and body language of different characters, as well as their interactions with other characters on the page and in the book. By doing this, we can model what sort of clues to observe when we wish to gauge someone's emotional state.

- *Explore different perspectives and build Theory of Mind*: Theory of Mind, ToM, is the ability to understand that the emotions, knowledge, desires and motivations of others will differ from one's own.

- *Develop an awareness of people in the wider world*: beginning to see them as individuals with personal stories and unique characteristics.

- *Communicate information about our own feelings*: describing how we view experiences, events, the world around us and the unfolding world within.

- *Build relationships*:

  - *Through the reciprocity of storytelling and reading, and the sense of intimacy it fosters*: Cox Gurdon (2019) quotes Susan Pinker, who in conversation described 'a tsunami of neurochemical benefits' that are 'unleashed when a parent and child cuddle together over a book… As soon as the parent puts his or her arms around the child, hormones flood their bloodstreams, relaxing them and engendering mutual trust' (p.47).

– *Through the shared emotional content*: Borba (2016) recounts the account of her reading of *Ramona the Pest* by Beverly Cleary to a class of first-grade children. In the class was a little girl called Molly whose father had deployed to Afghanistan the same week that she had started a new school. As Borba read about the character Ramona's possible leaving of her school due to feeling uncared for, Molly became increasingly focused on the story, evidently keenly feeling the emotions of Ramona. She whispered, 'It's okay, Ramona. Come back! You'll find a friend!' (p.81). Borba writes about how, on witnessing this, it was all she could do to keep focused on her reading of the story. But here is the heartwarming part. Molly's emotions had been noticed by another student, Annie, who was sitting nearby. As Borba describes it,

I caught Annie looking…at Molly; and then came the moment: her empathy was stirred. She knew Molly needed a friend, so she moved in a little closer and put her arm around her new buddy. Two girls listened together side by side, arm in arm. Here were two children in sync with a character's feelings as well as each other's, confirming what science says can happen with the right book at the right time. (2016, p.82)

– *Through the co-construction of stories*: children are constantly telling stories through their play. And even when at times they are not verbally narrating, their gestures will be acting out a story. It has been shown that children engage in this kind of symbolic play more and in richer ways when they do it with a facilitating adult, usually a parent or caregiver. A typical interaction consists of a young child moving a toy around, guiding the toy or toys through a sequence of actions. Often it is the adult who provides the language that highlights the narrative form embedded within the child's play gestures. Engel (2016) gives an example, a 22-month-old boy moving two figures on a tabletop and his father commenting as he plays, 'Oh look. Are those knights fighting… the green knight pierced the blue knight. Hurrah. Sir Greenie is the champion!' As we construct stories in this manner – always in partnership with children and with their permission, and alternating between following and leading them, we encourage increased expression of their imaginations, and we 'amplify their voices' (Engel 2016).

STORY AND COGNITION

Over the course of our lives, the cerebrum (which is the largest part of the brain) adapts itself to the world around us by fine-tuning itself. This is known as neuroplasticity. It is during early childhood that proliferation occurs – this is the creation of new synaptic and fibre tract connections – and this process is highly dependent on experiences like 'play, socialization and hearing stories read aloud' (Burns 2019). Novelty and reinforcement in our learning environments also cause neuromodulators like dopamine to be released, helping our brains to retain newly learned information permanently (ibid.).

On a cognitive level, story causes us to:

- *Develop attention and concentration.*

- *Organize experience:*

  - We use memory to tell stories from the past.

  - We work to understand and make sense of events, and how the world works in general.

  - We apply perspective taking in order to understand other people and relationships.

  - We consider cause and effect.

  - We hypothesize: what if?

  - We create alternative outcomes and endings through the evaluation of the plot.

- We learn to process abstract concepts.

- We use imagination: visualizing the story in our mind.

- *Increase vocabulary and formulate language to convey ideas*: Cox Gurdon (2019) uses a powerful analogy, describing words as 'keys that unlock the world' (p.95). She talks about how, in medieval times, the lady of a castle (the chatelaine) could be identified by the keys she carried, which enabled her to enter 'any chamber, any storeroom, any locked closet. Having the keys made her the mistress of the estate' (p.95). It is true that the more words children understand and use, the more access they have to knowledge. And it is this set of keys that will give them the ability to gain more. As Gurdon says, 'the more words they know, the more easily they'll pick up new ones from context, syntax and repetition' (p.95).

- *Construct a framework using basic information*:

  - Who are the characters?

  - What are the key events?

  - When did they occur?

  - How does the sequence unfold?

  - What is the perspective of the key characters?

  - What is the overall theme of the story?

  - What are the details you'd like to add?

- *Exercise working memory*: Working memory is the ability to keep information active in the mind for a short time to be able to use it for further processing, for example, holding the different elements of a story in mind as the plot unfolds.

- *Apply cognitive flexibility*: Cognitive flexibility refers to the brain's ability to move from thinking about one concept to another, revising plans in the face of new information, and adapting to changes in situations. This is often evident in children's imaginative play.

- *Build literacy skills*: According to a 2015 study carried out at the Cincinnati Children's Hospital Medical Center with children aged between 3 and 5, the effects of children being read to can be seen in their brain activity (Kemp 2015), with fMRI scans showing that 'when the young children were being told a story, a number of regions in the left part of the brain became active. These are the areas involved in understanding the meaning of words and concepts and also in memory' (Storrs 2016).

It is evident that stories have the potential to change our brains, engaging multiple cognitive functions as we become immersed in them. The question to ask is, 'Are these essential processes being engaged as we educate our children?'

Kieran Egan, writing in *Teaching as Story Telling – An Alternative Approach to Teaching and Curriculum in the Elementary School* (1986), says that:

Education, seen through the dominant planning and research models, is a largely logical and narrowly rational business. In this view, education is an area where there is little room for our emotional lives. For this reason, the 'affective' is usually considered a matter only for the arts – the educational margin or 'frills'. (p.29)

Indeed, we have witnessed this in educational planning in England over the past few years, with an increased focus on testing. This has resulted in raised levels of stress and lack of job satisfaction on the part of teachers, and a rise in mental health issues among children.

In an article titled 'Why English Schoolchildren Are So Unhappy' in the *New Statesman*, Tom Wigmore (2016) writes, 'Last year, a report by the National Union of Teachers found that 76 per cent of primary and 94 per cent of secondary school teachers felt that exams caused pupils to suffer from stress-related conditions.' Natasha Devon, appointed in August 2015 as the government's first ever champion for mental health in young people, warned: 'Children are tested rigorously from the age of four, with little or no creative outlet for their emotions in the form of sport and arts' (cited in Woolcock 2016). A survey of teachers in English state schools in 2018 reported that many of them expressed 'feeling that much of their work is meaningless' (Brady 2018).

We can contrast this educational approach with the deep meaning to be found in story, and the arts. As Egan (1986) says, the current dominant model of education has 'tended to suppress the affective aspects of learning. Consequently, they have drawn on only a divided part of children's learning capacities' (p.29). As practitioners and parents, we need to understand that affective meaning (the feelings awakened in readers by a text) is often what drives children's learning. It is this meaning that is important in terms of 'providing access to knowledge and engaging us in knowledge' (p.30) and it is through story that we can offer a more balanced approach to the teaching of young children.

HOW DO WE TELL STORIES?

In thinking about how we tell stories, we can begin to consider not only the manner in which we relay them (our methodology) but also the frequency of our story time with children and the openness with which we approach it. Indeed, the way that we tell stories is of vital importance, as it is the manner in which we approach them that will greatly influence whether children are intrigued and inspired or uninterested and therefore disengaged. In a 2020 study on emergent literacy led by Dr John Hutton at Cincinnati Children's Hospital, he witnessed 'an apparent "Goldilocks effect" when it comes to the way children respond to the modality of stories, with some kinds of storytelling being "too cold" for children, others being "too hot", and some "just right"' (Kamenetz 2018). The study consisted of 27 participants who were around 4 years old. The children were placed into an fMRI machine and monitored as they paid attention to stories that were presented in three different ways: 'audio only; the illustrated pages of a storybook with an audio voice-over; and an animated cartoon'. The machine scanned both for activation within certain brain networks, and connectivity between the networks.

The results showed that in the audio-only condition, while the language networks were activated, there was less connectivity overall, and evidently the children were straining to understand as they attended. In the animation condition, while activity was shown in the audio and visual perception networks, there was little connectivity among the various brain networks, and interestingly the children's comprehension of the story was the worst out of all three in this modality. The illustration condition was referred to by Dr Hutton as 'just right' (Kamenetz 2018). This was due to the fact that as the children could see the illustrations – although the language network activity declined slightly – their understanding was supported or 'scaffolded' by the images, which act as clues in terms of story comprehension. 'Most importantly, in the illustrated book condition, researchers saw increased connectivity between – and among – all the networks they were looking at: visual perception, imagery, default mode and language' (Kamenetz 2018).

Another interesting take away from the study is that Dr Hutton notes that the conditions of the illustration connection – although indicating they were optimal – weren't as good as when children are read to on the lap of a parent or someone who cares for them, which allows for physical contact and a close emotional bond, as well as the give and take of dialogic reading (where children are guided, prompted and asked questions, and pose questions of their own and help to tell the story).

Let's examine just a few of the methods we can use in order to cause our storytelling to be as effective as possible:

- Firstly, when considering the storytelling process, we can begin to view children not as passive recipients but as active partners in the process of story, offering their knowledge and stories up to us in response to our offering. We can make room for their responses, valuing their contributions. This accommodation may not allow for the strict observance of a lesson plan, but it is this interaction that makes story exciting – the fact that it takes on a life of its own, providing us with a springboard for further exploration of character traits, emotion, values and perceived difficulties. As we do this together, children will acquire confidence in terms of language and the expression of ideas, and feel accepted, affirmed and valued as their ideas are joyfully acknowledged. It is the confidence gained in these instances that will help them to speak up in group settings and in social situations, and later be able to express themselves in written form. (We can be unafraid of the meandering nature of story, gathering the children up again to come back to a salient point or learning objective, perhaps even stating a desire or making a note for the group to return to a subject of exploration or debate should time not allow for it. We can be honest with the children about our restrictions as they will appreciate our acknowledgement of their ideas and their desire to further explore them.)

- Secondly, we choose books that appeal to the children's interests. Early attention skills are the most consistent predictors of academic success, and attention has been shown to be enhanced through 'engaging with some novelty' (Burns 2019). Burns says that teachers can further enhance children's attention using simple methods like maintaining eye contact, moving and interacting with the children. A story is brought to life through animation: using body language, tone, gesture, etc. We can use expression – modulating our voices, matching our voice to the emotion expressed – for example speaking with a quaking voice when scared or laughing uproariously when something is humorous.

- Thirdly, we can create a comfortable, welcoming environment.

- We can read stories that are requested again and again, each time with the same degree of enthusiasm. Children often enjoy hearing the same story countless times and they begin to internalize it, making sense of it on a deeper level each time they hear it.

- We are accessible – sitting at the same level as the children if and when possible.

- We are relaxed with the children.

- We make room for representation – of different families, ethnicities, cultures, socio-economic backgrounds, etc. The world is diverse, and we allow for this diversity by accepting all children and all of their stories.

- We model thinking aloud – making connections for the children, considering the need to examine a story further: 'I wonder if this character is really who he says he is…can he be trusted?' This will teach children how to begin to evaluate narrative texts using critical thinking skills.

- We monitor understanding, checking that the children are following along with us as we tell or read, and retelling or re-reading certain parts of the story if required to ensure that they indeed are in sync with us.

- We try not to have strictly 'correct' answers in mind as the children answer. Of course, there are correct answers in terms of basic comprehension, but we can first allow the children time and space to think about the book and to offer up their initial thoughts and ideas. Indeed, it is often the case for us, as adults, that we need to re-read text or rewind a film to gain a better understanding of a story. At times, it is only after frequent exposure to a story that we begin to notice details, or understand concepts and themes that, at first, eluded us. Story is an immersive experience. We can begin by dipping in our toes, then venturing deeper and deeper. This form of exploration allows the children to soak up knowledge as the story washes over them time and again, rather than experiencing it as a sterile reading with questions fired at them afterwards in order to ascertain their comprehension. Mooney (2005, p.108) states that 'the wonder children bring to our classrooms can be snuffed out when we focus solely on our plan for children's learning rather than carefully listening to the children and following their conversational lead.' If we truly consider children as partners in the storytelling process, we will eagerly await their input and ideas, allowing them to speak to us as much as or even more than we speak to them.

- We can gently direct the children's attention to the most important illustrations, points and principles, asking questions like 'Did you see/notice?', 'Who can tell me more about…?' and 'Can you share your thoughts on…?'

- We can draw children's attention to the feelings of the characters, asking questions like 'How do you think the character feels?', and 'What clues can we follow to his/her feelings?'

- We lead them in examining feelings further – for example, asking them to imagine being the character, and to carefully consider what they might think, how they would feel, what actions they would consider taking and why.

- We formulate appropriate, open-ended questions that encourage further connection and reflection:

  - We think about ways of thinking, asking 'Would you think the same thing as the character?', 'What do you think about the character?' and 'What do you think about the story?' We can elaborate even further here (possibly with older children), asking 'What kind of thinking are you doing? Are you remembering? Comparing? Imagining? Planning?' There are countless ways in which to think, and we need children to begin to know and understand this.

  - We consider motivation and inspiration, asking 'What does the story make you feel you'd like to do?'

  - Carol Garhart Mooney in her 2005 book *Use Your Words: How Teacher Talk Helps Children*, says that divergent thinking skills are developed when we ask children questions like the ones above. She advises never to ask questions that we already know the answers to, and goes on to say that:

    One of the best ways that teachers can stimulate children's thinking and learning is asking good questions. Making statements instead of asking questions can sometimes put an end to a discussion that offers great possibilities for children to learn from each other or from their own misinformation. As teachers, our repertoire of questions is always in need of expansion and practice. (Mooney 2005, p.96)

  - We comment on differences in thinking, further developing Theory of Mind, for example, 'John likes the horses in the story, but Mary says she thinks horses are very big and a bit scary. She likes the cats.' We explain that others may often think and feel differently to the way that we do, and that these differences are acceptable. Our aim should be for children to feel comfortable with their own responses and confident in terms of expressing them, as well as being open to the contributions of others.

– We explore themes such as diversity, equality, purpose, struggle, resilience, hope, victory, compassion and empathy.

Cox Gurdon (2019) describes the act of reading together as securing 'people to one another, creating order and connection, as if we were quilt squares tacked together with threads made of stories' (p.47). This synchronization of brain activity is known as neural coupling, and Cox Gurdon cites Geoff Colvin, who explains it thus, 'We not only experience the story; we and the storyteller are having the same experience' (p.47). How utterly compelling is this knowledge. Not only are children connected to the person conveying a story, but they are also connected to their fellow listeners as they experience delight, sadness, anger, fear, uncertainty, wonder...a wide spectrum of emotions. The stories shared are then often played out individually or collaboratively with the information being further absorbed. And so we see that a singular story delivered by a teller has taken on a life of its own in the minds, hearts and play of the children. It has been considered and created anew on an individual level and it has functioned on a collective level, joining them together in a shared experience. It has addressed elements of their inner and outer worlds, all the while changing them. This is the dynamism of story.

Chapter 3

Story and Mathematics

DR JO VAN HERWEGEN

At first glance, it may appear as if mathematics and stories do not have much in common. Mathematics concerns itself with theory and facts while narratives can include fiction, fabricated characters and fantasy worlds. Recently, however, there has been an increased interest – including within the academic world – in the overlap between mathematics and narratives. This interest covers the mathematics of narratives: using mathematical ideas to study narrative techniques, the stories of mathematics teachers and the importance of narratives in teaching mathematics. When talking about the power of a story in a mathematical context, most people would consider stories from the history of mathematics – moments of great discovery or the political, social or physical struggles faced by many famous mathematicians. Think for example about John Nash in *A Beautiful Mind* or Katherine Johnson in *Hidden Figures*.

In considering our own mathematical stories and experiences, I'm sure that we will all agree that whether we like mathematics or not depends a great deal on the enthusiasm and the narratives of the maths teachers we encountered in our lives. Although the stories told by teachers can be worthwhile in embedding knowledge for students, there are other narrative processes that act as drivers of mathematical development from a young age.

Stories are powerful facilitators of learning for a number of reasons. People enjoy stories and stories can therefore help to motivate them to learn. Stories create more vivid, powerful and memorable images in a listener's mind which aid learning and recall of what has been learned. In addition, stories embed the concepts within a context, and this can make abstract concepts more accessible, or show how concepts can be applied in real life. In this chapter, I will provide an overview of why narratives may help young children to learn mathematics, drawing on recent research. The last part of this chapter will include additional practical tips for use by practitioners and parents.

THE BUILDING BLOCKS OF MATHEMATICS

Strong mathematical abilities are required for everyday living, and influence employability, wages and overall welfare. When talking about mathematics, many people think of counting and mathematical equations, or procedures such as addition and subtraction. However, mathematics is actually a complex notion that relies on a number of general cognitive abilities including good memory and the requisite attention to learn new things, as well as mathematical-specific knowledge and abilities.

Mathematical abilities start to develop in the womb when foetuses can hear sounds and feel rhythms (at around 24 weeks of gestation). Foetuses and infants often move when they get excited and recognize something as novel. Research has shown that foetuses will discriminate between different numbers of sounds or light that they experience in the womb. In certain studies, researchers played foetuses a number of sounds or showed them a number of infra-red lights through the womb. They then scanned the foetuses' movements. When the foetus was shown a new number of lights or was played a new number of sounds, the foetuses became active again and turned in the womb. Although foetuses cannot yet count, they have a feeling for numerosities that is called 'number sense'. Foetuses and infants can discriminate between small numbers including 1 to 3 sounds, objects or actions. It is thought that they use their memory system for this and map what they have seen or heard to a 'file' in memory. When they then see or hear a new number, they map the information in their memory to the number of things they observe. When the information in memory does not match the information presented to them this causes a surprise.

Infants from about 6 months of age can also discriminate between larger numerosities, such as 8 versus 16 dots, or 5 versus 10 jumps. Again, this ability is linked to their feeling for numbers or number sense. This number sense has been shown to be important for exact mathematics later in life, and it is thought to be a checking system for exact mathematics. A comparative adult example of number sense is when you add a batch of numbers using a calculator to get a total, but you suspect that something must have been wrong with your calculation as the total doesn't 'feel' right.

From the age of 18 months onwards, children will start learning to count. This usually begins with learning the number names and the order in which they progress. At this stage, children are not yet counting but rather reciting the number names, almost like a nursery rhyme. Once they have some number names, children will start to point and understand that when counting you need to count all of the objects in a set, one by one. However, children may not yet know what counting is for (i.e. to define the number of items in a set) and keep on counting, one by one, the items in a set twice or three times. Only when children have mastered 'cardinality', or the understanding that the number counted defines the number of items in that set, will children correctly count the items in a set and stop there, satisfied with their conclusion.

In addition to counting words, children also need to acquire a range of mathematical concepts, such as 'before', 'after', 'bigger', 'smaller', 'closer to', 'add', and 'subtract'. These mathematical words will help children to explain and describe numerical relationships and operations.

At a point in development, the symbolic counting information that children have acquired will come together with their number sense abilities. It is unclear yet how and when this takes place, but it has been argued that many people think about numbers in terms of a mental number line upon which numbers and their meaning are represented. The evidence that people have a mental number line comes from studies that have shown that when people in Western countries think about small numbers they often look at the left but when thinking about large numbers they look at the top right. In addition, when people in Western countries were asked which number out of two options on a screen is smaller, their responses were quicker when the smaller number was presented on the left of the screen as opposed to the right side of the screen. This is called the spatial-numerical association of response codes or SNARC-effect, which suggests that numbers are presented in a spatial presentation in our brains that has a left-to-right orientation in those who are raised within a Western culture and a right-to-left orientation for those whose language has a right-to-left orientation.

The mental number line allows for children's 'ordinality' or the knowledge of how numbers relate to each other (for example, knowing which number comes before 7 and which number follows 7) to develop, and these seriation abilities have been shown to be very important for children's mathematical success.

NARRATIVES AS AN ANCHOR FOR MATHEMATICAL DEVELOPMENT

Some think that learning is something abstract that happens in the brain. However, learning does not happen in isolation but rather in the context in which we use the concept. It is through continued situated use that meaning gets shaped, little by little. For example, learning the counting words and their meaning is one of the first steps in formal mathematical development. As described above, understanding the meaning of counting, or knowing that 'three' means a set with three things, is called cardinality. A central part of this counting process is the ability to recognize equivalence or knowing that multiple sets – even sets that differ along many dimensions – all belong to the same category by virtue of the number of items they contain. So three dogs, three sheep, three chickens and three cats are equivalent in that there are three in each group. Children learn this numerical equivalence concept gradually and across different contexts just like they learn the meaning of 'ball' and that there are different types of balls. Therefore, although books that show children pictures of sets of items might look very boring to adults, such books are very important to teach young children and infants the equivalence concept as well as the concepts of sets, and that sets have a defined number.

Picture books can represent mathematical concepts through their prose, illustrations, logical development and context. In addition, they provide excellent opportunities for engaging in rich mathematical discussions. Very young children can engage with quite sophisticated mathematical concepts if the context and tasks are appropriate.

An example that picture books can be powerful learning tools for young children comes from a study by Kinnear and Clark. Earlier studies that examined probabilistic reasoning (calculating the chances that something is likely to happen) in 6- and 7-year-old children had found that, although children were able to draw inferences from, when explaining their answers they would use subjective examples from their own experiences and showed little understanding of how they had achieved their answer. Kinnear and Clark (2014) then used a story picture book about a character called Litterbug Doug who, at first was very wasteful, but then learned about recycling and started to collect litter everywhere in the town. In their study, 5-year-olds were presented with the book along with a table of information about the rubbish that Litterbug Doug had collected on Monday, Tuesday and Wednesday, per type of item (e.g. five cans, two apple cores, three papers). Children were then asked to predict how much of each litter category Litterbug Doug would collect on Thursday. In contrast to previous studies that showed just data tables, children who were presented with the Litterbug Doug story drew exclusively from contextualized knowledge of the picture storybook to explain their predicted values when asked. This shows that children have the capacity and ability to draw meaningfully from data context knowledge to explain data observations if the connection to the data context source is meaningful.

Since narratives are an integral part of our everyday activities, and our counting system is a cultural notation that has evolved as a result of these everyday activities, it is not surprising at all to see that narratives are a powerful tool in helping children to develop mathematical abilities.

First, narratives can teach children new concepts and promote mathematical reasoning. Second, they contextualize mathematical ideas while engaging the child. Finally, they allow for rich discussions and wider exploration.

A study by Carrazza and Levine (2019) at the University of Chicago compared typical maths books that simply include sets of objects and books with the same objects and sets incorporated into stories (rich narratives) for numbers 1 to 10. They asked two groups of parents, one for the classic number books and one for the rich number stories, to use the books each day with their 3-year-olds. The researchers examined how well children could count and understand cardinality before they started using the books and after four days of using the books. Even though parents in both groups reported the same number of reading sessions during the four days, children in the rich narrative condition performed better on the cardinality and counting task than those who used the simple pictures of sets of objects. This shows that embedding knowledge into rich narratives aids children in learning mathematics faster.

Not only can the context help to embed knowledge and understanding; storybooks are also extremely useful in teaching children mathematical vocabulary. The development of mathematical vocabulary is important for young children as its use is necessary for them to reason and to understand maths. For example, when children learn that the words 'more' and 'less' can be used to describe numbers, they have a way to verbally explain the differences between a basket with ten apples in it and a basket with five apples in it. The use of storybooks that highlight mathematical vocabulary and explain numbers and how they relate to each other might help children 'mathematize' or understand everyday situations in mathematical terms.

We can see, then, that while the richness of narratives allows young children to learn concepts faster, and fosters a deeper understanding of mathematical vocabulary, there is evidence that even just reading books, whether they have a mathematical content or not, influences children's mathematical abilities.

As discussed above, it has been shown that people have an internal number line that goes from left to right in most Western countries, and it is thought that the direction of this number line is influenced by the reading direction in those countries. A recent study showed that when reading *The Very Hungry Caterpillar* by Eric Carle, a children's book in which the caterpillar comes out of an egg, looks for food and eats one apple, two pears, three plums, four strawberries and five oranges, children who read the book with the pictures presented from right to left but with page turning from left to right (i.e. the opposite of our Westernized system) changed their counting direction from right to left when counting a row of coins. Therefore, the orientation of the pages and pictures in shared book-reading activities can activate and change the child's spatial representation of numbers along a number line (see Göbel *et al.* 2018).

It has been shown that children who have a firm mental number line are more able to manipulate numbers and as a result have better mathematical abilities. Number lines and narratives share the fact that both have a structure or sequence to them. Therefore, using words such as 'before', 'after', 'in front', 'next', 'forwards' and 'backwards' in stories will help in the understanding of sequences and of number lines. In addition, books are like number lines, in that a book goes from page one to the final page just like a number line goes from the start to the finish. As pages are flipped, pages with smaller numbers are placed on the left and pages with larger numbers remain on the right. Therefore, as children become more familiar with books, they develop a stronger understanding of the relationship between space and numbers.

A study by O'Neill, Pearce and Pick (2004) examined the narratives of 3-year-old children who were asked to tell a story from a wordless picture book. The researchers analysed various aspects of the children's narratives, including how many conjunctions children used (i.e. sentences that include words such as 'and', 'but', 'or', 'because' and 'after'), along with the event content of the stories (namely, how many different parts the story contained, which shows the richness of the content of the story). The number of conjunctions and events used when children were 3 years old correlated to their mathematical performance at that age, as well as predicting their mathematical performance two years later. This suggests that there is a relationship between exposure to books, narratives and number line development, with improved number line abilities leading to improved mathematical abilities.

MATHEMATICS AND THE HOME ENVIRONMENT

Research has shown that number abilities in the preschool years are highly predictive of mathematical success in adulthood, and that children who enter preschool with strong counting and numeracy skills go on to excel in mathematics. Thus, developing a solid foundation in numeracy is crucial.

As discussed above, mathematical abilities start to develop early on, long before children start school and, indeed, research has shown that mathematical activities in the home, as well as parental mathematical skills and beliefs, can have an important influence on children's mathematical abilities. However, research has also shown that parents engage more frequently in literacy than numeracy activities with their children, and that this diminished frequency of activity is related to the parents' own confidence in relation to mathematical abilities. Those parents who do engage with mathematical activities with their young children often engage in counting activities while activities like using a ruler, working with money or creating equal-sized groups from a larger group generally occur less frequently. Yet, as discussed above, the use of a ruler can improve children's mental number line and thus children's mathematical potentiality.

When we consider early development, we need to keep in mind that it is not only formal and informal activities that can influence children's mathematical abilities. The amount and type of maths talk used during naturalistic conversations have also been shown to have an effect on children's mathematical development. A study by Susperreguy and Davis-Kean (2016) examined the instances of maths talk between mothers and their preschool children during mealtimes. The researchers found that those children who were exposed to more maths talk in naturalistic conversations during mealtimes showed higher levels of mathematical aptitude.

CHOOSING NARRATIVES

Although many of the studies discussed in this chapter examining relationships between narratives and mathematical abilities do not allow insight into the causal explanation for these relationships, several research studies have shown that systematic exposure to mathematics-related books can lead to greater interest in mathematics activities, deeper mathematics knowledge and more frequent use of mathematics vocabulary.

However, not all mathematical books are the same. There are stories that introduce concepts to children, stories that explain concepts, stories that ask questions and stories that embed knowledge in new areas. Therefore, it is important to consider what mathematical abilities your child already has when selecting books, and to introduce a variety of stories to improve mathematical skills across the board.

In addition, not all mathematical books are equally good. For example, picture books that focus on helping your child to count or learn counting names will often include simple pictures that form a set. But some picture books might be confusing for your child: it may not be clear whether the objects form one (picture A) or more sets (picture B), or what objects belong to a set as there may be a number of distractors (picture C).

Figure 3.1 Objects and sets

Books that include rhyme and repetition will help very young children and it is important that the number concepts appear in the correct order, rather than as a random presentation of numbers.

In order to support counting in children, it is important not only to label and count each object when counting; research by Mix *et al.* (2012) has shown that it is also important to first name the cardinal name of the set and then to count the number of items in the set. So, when counting four objects, go: 'Look, four! One, two, three, four.' This helps children better understand what counting is for.

As discussed above, books and activities that include narratives support mathematical development best. However, it is important to check that the background does not divert attention away from the concepts to be learned or items to be counted. When using a narrative approach (Russo and Russo 2017), it is best to start with choosing some favourite books and identifying the key characters and plot of the story. These stories can then be used to talk about mathematical concepts and applications in daily life.

Let's use the example of the children's favourite 'Goldilocks and the Three Bears'. This story is all about maths. The story starts with the introduction of Goldilocks, who goes for a walk in the forest and enters a house where she sees three bowls. This introduces the numerical concept of three and by circling the three bowls with your finger, children will be able to link the concept of three to the set size of three bowls. Some parents also count out the bowls by using one-to-one pointing. But the three bowls are not of equal size. There is a small, a medium and a large one, therefore teaching children the concept of size. The sequence of the number three and the three different sizes is repeated within the book in discussing the bowls, chairs and beds of the three bears. This repetition allows the child to gain a deeper understanding of how the number three is always the same across different contexts (the concept of equivalence discussed earlier on).

A less well-known but lovely story is 'Two of Everything' by Lily Toy Hong, a Chinese folktale that tells the story of poor farmers Mr and Mrs Haktak. They find a large cookery pot with strange powers: it doubles everything placed in it! The Haktaks become wealthy by repeatedly placing money in the pot and taking out twice as much. However, one day Mrs Haktak falls into the pot and Mr Haktak is faced with two wives instead of one. On another day, Mr Haktak also falls in the pot. The new Haktaks all become friends and live together. This story introduces the child to the concept of 'two' and 'double' and can then provide the background to further discuss times tables.

In reality, all books and stories contain some kind of mathematical content, as mathematics is truly embedded in our culture: telling the time, reading the number of a bus/train to catch, postcodes, telephone numbers, cooking, etc. Therefore, it is less about the kind of book used but rather about how books can be used to highlight mathematical concepts.

The best way to teach children mathematical concepts is to first read the story while pointing out pictures and highlighting mathematical concepts and vocabulary words such as 'same', 'different', 'bigger', 'smaller', 'half', 'whole', 'next', 'after' and 'before'. We often assume that children will implicitly absorb the information we tell or teach them. Although this is true to some extent, it is better to talk to children about the vocabulary words and define them within the context of the story. For example, when reading the story 'Two of Everything', a child might not be familiar with the word 'double' and thus it may be necessary to explain this explicitly. In order to check that the child has understood the mathematical concept in the story you could ask for some other examples of the mathematical concept from the book or even from outside the book. For example, when reading 'Goldilocks' you can say, 'There were three bowls in the book' and then ask 'Were there any other groups of three?'

In conclusion, mathematical learning begins at birth and is fostered in the home environment. Through narratives and shared book reading, children develop an improved mathematical understanding which can influence their mathematical abilities later in life. There are a number of ways in which narratives can help children. First, narratives can teach children new concepts such as counting, number words and cardinality. Second, books and narratives provide a structure and sequence that may influence children's mathematical number line visualization and understanding of how numbers relate to each other. Third, narratives and books facilitate children's development of a rich mathematical vocabulary. And, finally, books and narratives help to engage children and to provide a rich context in which mathematical concepts and ideas can be applied, which allows for deeper mathematics knowledge.

Table 3.1 Resources for mathematical narratives

Title	Author	Concepts
Baby Goes to Market (2018)	Angela Brooksbank	Counting, Addition, Subtraction
Have You Seen My Dragon? (2015)	Steve Light	Counting
Sheep Won't Sleep (2018)	Judy Cox, illustrated by Nina Cuneo	Counting by 2s, 5s and 10s
Absolutely One Thing (2017)	Lauren Child	Number Line, Calculations, Digit Recognition
Two Greedy Bears (1998)	Mirra Ginsburg	Divide, Equal, Part/Whole, Piece, Bigger/Smaller, Half
McElligot's Pool (1947)	Dr Seuss	With/Without, Short/Long, Bigger/Smaller, Add/Subtract
Caps for Sale (1940)	Esphyr Slobodkina	First/Second/Third, Above/Below, Before/After
Harold and the Purple Crayon (1955)	Crockett Johnson	Straight, Short/Long, None, More than/Less than, Left/Right
Olivia (2000)	Ian Falconer	Enough, Before/After, Closer to, Add/Subtract
Mike Mulligan and His Steam Shovel (1939)	Virginia Lee Burton	Some, As many as, Least/Greatest, Part/Whole, Add/Subtract

cont.

Title	Author	Concepts
The Snowy Day (1962)	Ezra Jack Keats	Equal, Before/After, Add/Subtract, More/Less, Pair
The Greedy Triangle (2008)	Marilyn Burns	Shapes and Angles, Counting
The Doorbell Rang (1989)	Pat Hutchins	Dozen, Division

SUGGESTION FOR FURTHER READING

Muir, T., Livy, S., Bragg, L., Clark, J., Wells, J. and Attard, C. (2017) *Engaging with Mathematics Through Picture Books*. Albert Park: Teaching Solutions.

Chapter 4

Exploring Language and Cognition

DR VALERIE LOVEGREEN

Truth be told, everyone loves a good story. Whether the story is told to us, told by us, read to us or read by us, stories cause us to think, allow us to use language and deepen our connections with others. In using stories we remember the past, describe the present and look to the future.

Everyone has a story. Stories are a way for us to show our life's journey. They provide us with ways in which to share the smaller, daily happenings that are meaningful to us. And stories move beyond cultures, showing us how we differ from each other, and how we are the same.

Stories are often called narratives. When we tell stories about ourselves or about others, it is because we think they are important. These are defined as personal narratives. When we make up a story with characters, events and experiences that are not based in reality, these are regarded as fictional narratives.

Young children tell wonderful stories. Many of us may have experienced a young toddler, with emerging language skills, attempting to share an experience. The joyful sharing of early years children can be a delight to behold, and the sorrows expressed provide us with an opportunity to acknowledge, calm and comfort. These burgeoning shared stories improve thinking and speaking skills and teach children how to reflect and how to interact with those around them.

We are familiar with storytellers. But do we ever think about story listeners? As we consider both, we can ask ourselves some questions in order to better understand the two parts of story:

- How do storytellers create a narrative?

- How do story listeners 'listen' to a story?

- What makes 'telling' an important part of the experience?

- What makes 'listening' an important part of storytelling?

- How do we know that the 'listening' skills and 'telling' skills worked?

- If a child's storytelling or story listening is not effective, what can we as parents and teachers do about it?

Understanding both sides of the story, the telling and the listening, helps adults to teach children about stories and provides us with a chance to gain insight into children's thinking processes.

TYPES OF COMMUNICATION AND WHERE STORY FITS IN

In this chapter we will learn about the elements of story and discover what it takes to tell and listen to a story in terms of our thoughts and the language we choose to use. As parents and teachers, we have a responsibility to model and teach both how to tell a story and how to listen to one.

A narrative is one of four components of discourse, parts of written or spoken communication; and each component is considered to be important because developing skills in all four areas can improve literacy skills, social skills and communication (Bliss and McCabe 2008).

Table 4.1 Genres of discourse

Conversation – talk between or among people	Scripts – descriptions of routines
Expository – describing or explaining a topic or concept	Narrative (two types): personal – a story of personal experience fictional – a made-up story

Conversation

We all experience conversation or talk between two or more people. But have you ever thought about what you do when you speak and what you do when someone else is speaking? What makes a conversation successful? The speaker is responsible for providing information and for making sure it makes sense to the listener. The listener is responsible for paying attention and adding information that relates to the topic.

Scripts

Scripts describe routine activities. An example is when we tell children to get ready for bed and we mention brushing teeth, putting on pyjamas, etc. The information is not new but rather is familiar to both the speaker and the listener (Bliss and McCabe 2008).

Expository discourse

Expository discourse describes or explains a topic, for example in subjects like science and social science. In expository discourse the 'teller' must share accurately and in a logical sequence so that the listener or reader will understand the information (ibid.).

Narratives

Last, we have narrative discourse, of which there are two types, personal and fictional.

Personal narratives are used to share information about self or others in social interactions. In a personal narrative, the speaker describes their view of what happened to themselves and others, shared as actual experiences from the past and present. Personal narratives tend to be longer and more involved than conversation or free play interactions (ibid.).

Fictional narratives are pretend stories, created by the storyteller. There is a structure to these narratives, which helps the storyteller to organize and present the story, and it helps the story listener to follow and understand the narrative. Some of the stories we read and the stories that we generate in our imaginations are fictional narratives (ibid.).

Table 4.2 Narrative

Personal	Fictional
Tell about a real past event	Creation or recall of story
Real events	Imagined events
Often involve social experiences	Often created in school assignments

In creating a narrative, someone creates or shares the story, and someone receives the story. A story narrative is based on something that happened, and for the storyteller the experience shifts from 'being' an experience to the 'telling' of an experience. In analysing how to engage children with story we think about what gets the listener's attention and what moves the speaker to share (Labov 2006; Mäkinen *et al.* 2014).

We can begin by looking at the thinking and language used in both creating and listening to a narrative. As these narratives form a part of children's play, socializing and literacy, and since narratives build thinking, language and emotional development skills, it is essential that we identify how it is that parents and teachers can help the development of narrative skills in the lives of children.

THE LANGUAGE AND COGNITION COMPONENTS OF NARRATIVE: WORDS, SENTENCE STRUCTURE, SOCIAL INTERACTIONS

As we have seen, narrative development begins early and continues over our lifespan. Our personal narrative changes from birth to death based on our experiences and is formed by the culture in which we grow up, in terms of family, community and nation. As adults, there are many ways to support children's narrative development when we keep these basic ideas in mind.

Begins early in development and continues into early adulthood

Narrative competence develops between the ages of 2 and 6

Between 3 and 6 (preschool and kindergarten years) – greatest development

Greatest narrative development occurs between the ages of 3 and 6 (with age comes increased linguistic and cognitive skill – contributing to longer and more complex narrations)

Through to age 9 – continued development with increased complexity and abstraction

Continued development between the ages of 6 and 9 (with increased complexity and abstraction)

Inspired by Ahn 2012; Khan *et al.* 2016; Labov 2006; Mäkinen *et al.* 2014

Figure 4.2 Narrative development

All cultures pass on their traditions through their stories (Panc, Georgescu and Zaharia 2015). Stories can be created, told, written, proclaimed, read, practised and acted out by humans, often contributing to teaching and learning (Sisk-Hilton and Meier 2017). Story is an integral part of Indigenous cultures and is used to help young children know themselves and others, as a way to share family history and in supporting the development of listening skills, the ability to interpret information and the capacity to reflect when thinking (Iseke 2013). In Canada, oral storytelling is seen as integral to the development of literacy in First Nations early years children (McKeough *et al.* 2008) and in Australia, links between oral stories and the development of literacy skills is also evident (Dunn 2001).

Zero to three years

Children begin to create narratives at an early age (Levy and McNeill 2015), with storytelling development paralleling language development at around age 2 (Engel 2016).

LANGUAGE

Children are beginning to put words together to make sentences, and these combinations can be used to describe characters, actions and events, all parts of a narrative. Stories contain language and cultural elements as children find meaning in communicating with others and learn about their family's culture (Sisk-Hilton and Meier 2017). Stories are shared through interactions with others and, for very young children, narrative can be the start of learning how to explain ideas and events and share personal experiences, prompting the development of communication skills and social interaction.

Story building requires skill with the 5 Ws and the knowledge of how to sequence information in time and space (Walsh *et al.* 2011). The 5 Ws are 'who', 'what', 'where', 'when' and 'why', and we can also add 'how'. At an early age, the who and the what are important Ws, and we can model using 'who and what', and listen and support children's use of them in stories.

We can use voice inflection, facial expressions, gestures and body language to teach children about these features of a story (Mokhtar, Halim and Kamarulzaman 2011). Learning to pay attention to and understand these devices will help children to begin to develop story understanding and pave the way for comprehension of more complex stories in the future.

COGNITION

The essence of the story reflects the thoughts of the mind (Mokhtar *et al.* 2011). It is always fun and exciting to learn about what very young children are 'thinking' about and, as they develop language, we can begin to know what their thoughts are. These thoughts can begin to be expressed as stories, as young children listen to stories and begin to relate and then to communicate their life experiences. Bruner (1990) believes that children are born with the ability to tell a narrative. Through narratives, children begin to experience how people, information and events are connected. They begin to understand the links between what they see, hear, feel and do and how these experiences affect others.

Listening to and telling narratives allows young children to begin to think about what emotions are, and it has been found that children are better able to identify emotions in a story than when observing a person's facial expressions (Widen, Pochedly and Russell 2015). This development may occur because stories are contextualised, offering support or scaffolding for the building of these types of thinking skills.

The early years

LANGUAGE

Between the ages of 3 and 6, language and narrative skills gain pace (Khan *et al.* 2016). Children lengthen their sentences and increase their vocabulary, both in conversations and in narratives. Sentences become more complex as children learn to link information and begin to understand cause and effect. Children build a storehouse of words that they can understand and use. Stories become longer and more descriptive as children engage in play with others, and adults begin to ask more questions, thereby challenging and enhancing children's thinking and language skills.

There is a developmental progression in storytelling development (Stadler and Ward 2005). When young children begin to tell stories, they simply name items and then list information. Later, they learn to sequence information because their understanding and use of language is expanding, and this development leads to improved narrative ability.

Story building continues by adding more of the 5 Ws, and sequencing in time and space (Walsh *et al.* 2011). The development of 'who' and 'what' expands, and we see 'where' and 'when' begin to emerge. At this stage children can begin to learn to create narratives using language and thinking that is decontextualized, meaning that they do not have to be in the concrete space and time to relate information (Nicolopoulou, McDowell and Brockmeyer 2006). They can think back to the past and will also begin to think towards the future to create ideas and to generate information not in the here and now. Since involvement in stories commonly involves interactions with others, as narrative ability develops, children become better able to explain their ideas, discuss events and share personal experiences. Narratives serve not only to inform but also to regulate information, build social relationships and construct avenues through which to share troubles or accomplishments (Walsh *et al.* 2011).

All narratives have a framework with basic parts including characters, settings, events, goals, attempts, outcomes and possible resolutions. This framework provides a predictable schema, which the storyteller and story listener can follow, akin to a road map (Khan *et al.* 2016). Each part is represented with some element of language – either a noun, verb, adjective or adverb – along with connecting words which are combined to create the story. Connecting words link events, create cohesion and contribute to the meaning of the storyline; these connectors help the storyteller to organize the time and space elements of the narrative and help the story listener to track the components to create a cohesive experience (Levy and McNeill 2015).

Vocal inflection, facial expressions, gestures and body language can also continue to be used in a fun, non-threatening atmosphere (Mokhtar *et al.* 2011). Gestures contribute to establishing a cohesive story and add a dynamic perspective that helps the storyteller to tell the story and the story listener to understand the story from the perspective of the storyteller (Levy and McNeill 2015). Gestures and speech together provide support for young children who are sharing a narrative (Stites and Özçalışkan 2017). Over time and with development, the gestures fade as the language and thinking skills improve.

COGNITION

Stories define us and tell who we are and how we fit into the world (Sisk-Hilton and Meier 2017). The ability to produce a narrative develops between the second and sixth year, requiring the use of inner speech, the ability to develop ideas, problem-solve and share information (Ahn 2012). Inner speech is the information that you 'discuss' with yourself to work through problems, make plans or sequence information; it helps to develop abstract thinking which is necessary for later learning in school. Children at this stage are beginning to think about more involved stories, as stories increase in length and richness of ideas.

Young children learn how to understand time and space with personal narrative development (Miller, Chen and Olivarez 2014). As children think about the 'when' and 'where' parts of their story, they begin to connect ideas.

Young children tend to repeat their narratives, allowing them to change their story, watch the listener for a response and then practise different versions to discover the many ways a narrative can develop and impact the listener. Children begin to connect story with their emotions, to learn about the emotions of others and to see that emotions are linked to facts, then move towards solutions (Miller *et al.* 2014). The repetition of narratives and these connections lead to the development of logical thinking and therefore solution-oriented thinking.

Storytelling has been shown to develop:

- verbal fluency

- verbal expression

- non-verbal expression

- self-confidence

- reading comprehension

- recognition of emotions

- teamwork.

(Panc et al. *2015)*

The early school-age years

LANGUAGE

Again, narrative and language development parallel each other because children continue to expand their sentence length and vocabulary, and their narratives become increasingly complex and abstract (Khan *et al.* 2016). Both personal and fictional narratives are important at this stage. Children are involved in making friends with classmates and so the sharing of personal information in a narrative becomes important. Children are listening to fictional narratives that are read to them, and they are often asked to answer comprehension questions that may require 'a correct answer'. They therefore need to understand how fictional stories work.

Oral language must be accurate so that the listener understands the speaker, and the storyteller must connect the characters in space and time. These skills are critical to reading comprehension throughout life (Stadler and Ward 2005). In listening to a story children must develop the ability to perceive and process the narrative, then comprehend the information and possibly problem-solve. In writing stories children must understand story parts such as characters, settings, actions and reactions because these elements must be used in narrative construction. The academic demands of the classroom limit the time and opportunities for storytelling and story listening so it is crucial that every opportunity that can be provided for narrative practice is seized, as it is this practice that will help children's thinking and language skills to develop (Sisk-Hilton and Meier 2017).

Practice in creating narratives helps children to further develop decontextualized language and thinking, where children can tell stories without having to be in the moment when the experience occurred. Conversations do not allow for the extensive development of decontextualized language and thinking as much as narrative does (Nicolopoulou *et al.* 2006). Through narrative children learn to think about information from the past and to predict what may happen in the future.

Narrative helps with verbal expression skills in much the same way, by supporting the development of the ability to respond with vocabulary and sentences of increasing length, complexity and abstraction. Narrative promotes discussion, which allows opportunities to learn how to discuss topics (Belet and Dal 2010).

COGNITION

Story comprehension and story expression are valuable skills, necessary in learning and throughout life (Moreau 2010). In all conversations and story narratives, the speaker and the listener must be able to take the perspective of others, analyse the characters and their actions, identify emotions and decide why characters do what they do (Moreau 2010). Creating and listening to narratives offers children the opportunity to experience and learn how to discover different points of view. Self-confidence grows with practice in self-expression. Children begin to develop an awareness of their own perspective from the reactions of others and begin to know how and when to defend their position and when to change their perspective (Belet and Dal 2010).

Between the ages of 3 and 5, children struggle to present and track stories clearly; however, by the age of 6, children begin to master this skill, and their narratives become longer and more abstract without the need for any gestural supports (Stites and Özçalışkan 2017). Storytelling during primary school years improves reading skills. When listening skills and speaking skills develop, they positively impact pre-literacy and literacy skills, and reading skills improve because story sharing promotes discussion, generates curiosity and allows students to learn how to ask and answer questions (Belet and Dal 2010).

Personal narratives continue to develop over time, but they do not begin to become coherent until early adolescence, when children have a firm understanding of time and space, and cause and effect (Vlaicu and Voicu 2013). Applebee (1977) describes the stages of narrative, providing helpful information for both parents and teachers to understand the growth and development of language, thinking and narrative skills.

Figure 4.3 The stages of personal narrative

In the first stage, children tell *heap stories*, as they are heaped together in an unorganized collection and their skills are limited to describing events and actions with no themes to their narrative. In Stage 2, they begin to be able to *sequence* these events and actions, but there is no story plot. In Stage 3, a *primitive* or beginning narrative occurs and includes events, actions and results of the action. By Stage 4, children can link or *chain* the events in planning their story, and they include character motivations for their actions, but the plot is still weak.

By Stage 5, children can tell *true narratives* with all of the parts that are understood and enjoyed by others.

In general, the better students are at oral stories, the better they are with written stories (Bigozzi and Vettori 2016). In the end the goal is for children to be competent, in telling and writing 'classically structured' narratives (Bliss and McCabe 2012). We can greatly aid in their school success by helping them to develop the ability to tell a coherent personal narrative and to understand and create fictional narratives.

HOW PARENTS AND TEACHERS CAN HELP DEVELOP CHILDREN'S NARRATIVE

Both parents and teachers can support narrative development in children. Storytelling entertains and can be a joy at home and a tool for teaching in the classroom. It supports the development of eye contact, attention, comprehension and problem solving (Mokhtar *et al.* 2011). As a learning instrument, storytelling helps children to learn how to express themselves, be imaginative, and discover and think about the emotions of self and others (ibid.).

The art of telling and the art of listening to support narrative development

Famous psychologist Lev Vygotsky's theory of play included narrative, and he suggested the idea that story development is important in childhood. In imaginary play, children learn about the rules of story-telling, which improves their understanding of rules when interacting with others (Nicolopoulou *et al.* 2015). In play children learn that there are speakers and listeners, and that each play a role in successful play and story building.

The storyteller has a story to share, has a certain view of a situation, organizes the parts of the story and shares. The story listener can play many roles: silent partner, supporter, commentator, evaluator, a supplier of information and all-round cheerleader. As adults we can choose how to support and teach listening. Too often we choose to evaluate and supply information, when the child's story and the child's self-esteem might benefit from a silent partner or supporter. Sometimes children can figure things out by themselves, given a little time and space, with some cheerleading at the end for being successful. The most ideal scenario is when children tell stories to adults who listen, responding with empathy, asking for clarification and valuing the process (Cattanach 2008).

Supporting development through shared story reading

Shared reading stimulates the brain and enhances language, executive function and social-emotional skills (Hutton *et al.* 2017). Shared story reading teaches children how to work together and supports the understanding of events, actions and emotions through the use of words (Mokhtar *et al.* 2011). Storytelling can have a positive effect on academic learning and social skill development (Liu *et al.* 2010).

Supporting development through shared listening and talking

We have learned that story listening and telling provide opportunities to improve language, thinking and social skills. Stories also provide opportunities for children to realize that other people may think differently to how they think. Stories help children to identify relationships of cause and effect and connections between stories and real-life experiences. And, maybe most importantly, the development of narrative goes hand in hand with the development of empathy (Belet and Dal 2010).

Teachers can use shared story time to practise helping children to learn how to listen. They can share the rules for when to talk, improving the ability to take part in social situations. These oral story-sharing experiences provide opportunities to practise empathy, and the viewing of situations from multiple perspectives. Shared storytelling is rich with opportunity. However, teachers and parents must take care not to make the interactions too overpowering or repetitive because children may feel overwhelmed or bored and lose interest (Belet and Dal 2010). The children should not feel 'talked at' but rather 'talked with'. The shared experience should create new experiences, build upon the ideas of others and produce a story where adults and children feel a sense of connection, contribution and accomplishment. As children listen, they begin to understand the elements of a story. As children talk in combination with teachers to create a story, they learn to produce the elements of cohesive, informative and interesting stories. And the fun is in the sharing!

Supporting development through shared reading and writing activities

Parents and teachers can support four skills that are necessary for what is termed 'critical reading'. These skills are:

- Questioning – questions are powerful tools for teaching and learning; they can stimulate thinking and advance language skills, and teach reasoning and problem-solving.

- Prediction – making predictions can encourage thinking and learning (Brod, Hasselhorn and Bunge 2018).

- Discussion – the back-and-forth interplay between speaker and listener stimulates higher-level thinking and precise language use.

- High-level thinking skills and asking critical questions – critical questions can lead to more effective critical thinking (Cojocariu and Butnaru 2014).

Parents and teachers can promote the development of personal and fictional narratives

Adults know how to create and how to retell stories. Modelling both types of narratives will help children to learn how to listen to stories and show children how stories start, develop along the way and come to an end.

Narratives include characters, settings, events, goals, attempts, outcomes and endings, and parents can show children how to include these parts in their narratives by modelling and asking questions that help children add information to make their stories rich and accurate. Create characters and talk with children about how you created the characters. The same structure can be used to discuss the other parts, including how you describe a story's setting, how you sequence happenings, set goals, handle success or disappointment and how you end the story. Wordless picture books can serve as a wonderful way to model and teach the parts of a story. (McConnell 2011)

PROMOTING PERSONAL NARRATIVES

Personal narratives are stories of real-life experiences, often heard in the spontaneous interactions of early years students. These opportunities allow children to learn how to make connections with others and develop friendships (Bliss and McCabe 2012).

When we tell stories to others we learn about ourselves (Cattanach 2008). Families tell stories and as children listen to the stories told by family members they begin to see the parts of a story (ibid.). From a young age, possibly as young as 2 years, children begin to listen to and participate in family stories, about where they live, who they are in the family and what traditions their culture holds (ibid.). These personal narratives are told, retold and evolve, and sometimes they disappear entirely. By the end of the early years, children can tell a narrative about their personal experiences. Adults can continue to help with these personal narratives by modelling and encouraging young children to talk about the past and the present, and to make predictions about the future (Miller *et al.* 2014).

Parents and teachers can support students in creating personal narratives, allowing children to practise maintaining a topic and explore sequencing, and guide them in knowing how to smoothly tell an interesting story (Bliss and McCabe 2012). The smooth relaying of a story relies on the ability of the storyteller to track the characters and help the listener know who did what to whom, when, where and how (Stites and Özçalışkan 2017). This task is challenging for young children and develops over time, often with this adult support.

Adults can share parts of their personal story as a model for children and can also point out events that happen in the child's personal narrative and help them to learn to share these with others (Miller *et al.* 2014). To share a personal narrative, children will need to develop an understanding of time and space, and teachers can help with this development through modelling and providing examples for children (ibid.).

Much of a child's personal narrative may be revealed during play with friends and so parents and teachers can offer many opportunities for play and help children to share about themselves during these moments. Social interactions may indeed require the sharing of personal narratives, so when teachers promote a child's sharing of personal experience, they are contributing to the child's present and future social development (Bliss and McCabe 2008).

PROMOTING FICTIONAL NARRATIVES

Fictional narratives include stories that are created and stories that are retold. These stories can be told through oral storytelling, by making stories from pictures or by reading books with words. Both methods of telling stories can improve children's comprehension and ability to create a fictional story.

To support the development of children's oral stories, teachers can scribe them, placing ideas on paper, which is a powerful experience for children. In the 1990s Vivian Gussin Paley developed the storytelling and story-acting practice (STSA) where children create stories, and adults act as scribes, recording the children's words. These same stories are then read aloud and acted out. In this activity children realize that stories are important, they can be written, they can be shared with others and they can be retold and re-enacted many times (Nicolopoulou *et al.* 2015). Children can also be encouraged to draw their ideas, which helps to develop setting and character creation, and also teaches the sequencing of story parts.

Shared stories created by teachers and children can be a powerful way to learn how to understand and create stories. Individual and group stories can develop many skills necessary for academic success. Indeed the sharing of stories in this way builds and expands oral language, emergent literacy and social skills. Collaborative story generation builds both thinking and language skills that will support enhanced reading comprehension later in life (Nicolopoulou *et al.* 2015).

Another useful resource that aids in promoting fictional narratives is a resource like a 'Storysack'. Storysacks were developed by Neil Griffiths in the 1990s. The adult–child interaction around a Storysack allows the child to experience the creation and telling of a story with support from the props contained therein. Children learn to develop meaning from these experiences and can begin to speak about what matters to them and to explore new ideas and new emotions (Barron and Powell 2002).

Since narratives have a structure of characters, settings, events, goals, attempts, outcomes and possible resolutions, teachers can use this structure to teach how to create a story (Khan *et al.* 2016). Both personal and fictional narratives share this structure. Teachers can decide which parts are troublesome for the child and support development in this area. Teachers can assess the areas that are not as strong as others and choose to model and/or talk about them with the children so that they can enhance their skills. Children may need support to learn to:

- add structure using 'beginnings, middles and ends in stories'

- sequence events

- add cause and effect

- evaluate the consequences in the story

- make the story believable

- describe the perspectives of the characters

- end a story, bringing it to a conclusion.

(adapted from Blom and Boerma 2016; Labov 2006)

Read aloud to support narrative development

Studies show that listening while reading increases word knowledge (Valentini *et al.* 2018). Reading to children enhances so many skills that are valuable in school and in life. And reading stories to children is fun. There is such joy in reading along and watching children's reactions and hearing their responses to the story action.

How we read or tell stories has an effect on comprehension and supports helping children to understand the purpose of stories. When an experience is enjoyable children want to do it again, and they will model that experience. As adults we must think about how we read or tell stories. When we pace the story and allow time for children to reflect, both during and after the story, they are able to connect with the experience and may remember the information, reason about the situation and use the knowledge in the future. Children love to ponder and wonder, but too many questions or questions that are repetitive or fast paced may tend to reduce the joy of the experience. Sometimes a simple pause or one open-ended question such as, 'Well, what did you think…?' maintains the joy and allows the child to think and use language to respond in a way that is fun for all.

Model writing to support narrative development

When children see adults writing stories they realize the value inherent in the process and will learn how writing a story happens. Adults can begin with drawings, which can show how stories have a sequence, with a clear beginning, middle and end. When adults or children tell stories, and someone takes the time to write them down, this reinforces the value of the written word.

As the child tells a story, the adult can write what the child does and says, then read it back to the child, and they can begin to refine the story based on their shared experience (Pack 2016). In this way a personal connection is built, and reciprocity is fostered as they work together and share in the joy of story creation.

Development is more than answering questions or recalling facts

Questions, predictions, discussions, reasoning, problem solving and critical thinking are all parts of a narrative. Reading stories with these elements in mind can guide teachers when asking questions. In reading stories to children, teachers can formulate questions and comments that will support the development of these skills.

When adults ask questions and make comments, they are modelling a shared experience in which children can participate. Through this modelling children learn the skill and importance of asking good questions and commenting on the happenings in stories. Reading stories and writing stories together with children affords teachers and parents the opportunity to model skills, comment on children's skills and teach to improve the skills. The ability to question, predict, discuss and ask critical questions contributes to the development of all types of communication and sets children up for future academic success.

NARRATIVE AS A VALUABLE LEARNING TOOL

Storytelling is considered to be an art – one that transcends cultures, is part of every society and is available to human beings of all ages (Mokhtar *et al.* 2011; Nicolopoulou *et al.* 2015; Sisk-Hilton and Meier 2017). Narratives help children and adults to interpret their daily experiences (Bruner 1990). In addition to improving and expanding language skills and enhancing thinking skills, the ability to produce a strong narrative helps in the development of pre-literacy skills and social skills and helps children to develop empathy for others. Children who can develop narratives are able to comprehend stories and factual information (Ahn 2012). Their skills of reasoning, problem solving and prediction are strong, which sets them up for success in the classroom and in life (Nicolopoulou *et al.* 2015). When children's verbal expression skills are developed, they are able to explain themselves fully and to ask for what they need. There is clarity in their communication. These skills are also strong predictors that they will be successful in later life (Bliss, McCabe and Miranda 1998). Finally, the ability to listen to and to share narratives develops curiosity and imagination (Cremin, Chappell and Craft 2013). This curiosity and creativity, along with critical thinking abilities, are important for success in school and for thriving in our global twenty-first century.

REMINDERS REGARDING THE ART OF STORY

When adults paint a picture of a story for the listener, children learn how to mentally picture the story and will learn to develop narrative skills and will in turn paint pictures of their own. Through storytelling, children learn how to organize information in sequence, a valuable tool for school and in life. Our stories can help build empathy in children, who will then create stories with empathy, making healthy connections with others. And, finally, good stories flow, and children learn how life flows, developing the ability to listen to the stories of others, create their own stories and develop connections with others through shared stories. Through this shared narrative process children gather the skills and perspectives necessary for lifelong learning and connections.

Chapter 5

Stories and Healing

Stories can extend a lifeline to children living through loss, loneliness, deprivation or trauma, providing comfort, acting as a roadmap for children who grow up in an environment that is morally or spiritually deficient, and offering a rich variety of experience to children who are culturally deprived. Indeed, through books, children are able to access not only their own culture but the cultures of many others. In her letter for the book *A Velocity of Being: Letters to a Young Reader* (Popova and Bedrick 2018), Rebecca Solnit writes of her experience of books in childhood, describing them as: 'bricks, not for throwing but for building'. She explains how she used them, saying:

> I piled the books around me for protection and withdrew inside their battlements, building a tower in which I escaped my unhappy circumstances. There I lived for many years, in love with books, taking refuge in books, learning from books a strange data-rich out-of-date version of what it means to be human. Books gave me refuge. Or I built refuge out of them, out of these books that were both bricks and magical spells, protective spells I spun around myself. They can be doorways and ships and fortresses for anyone who loves them.

Bessel van der Kolk, the prominent neuroscientist and trauma specialist, agrees with Solnit's description of stories as a protection and escape, saying that:

> A large number of survivors of childhood trauma, who I know, were avid readers as kids. They were terrified, abandoned, and continuously exposed to violence, and yet they found Harry Potter or Jane Austen. They disappeared in the stories. The imaginary worlds generated by

other people allowed them to create alternate universes to the ones they were living in. (van der Kolk 2015a)

Indeed, it is not only the stories read, watched or learned that can provide sanctuary and healing. When we witness the stories of people around us: lives of freedom, courage and peaceful ways of being, these very real, active stories can lead us to believe in the attainability of a different way of being. And these stories are everywhere if we search for them.

Esfahani Smith in *The Power of Meaning* (2017) discusses research showing 'that fiction can help people who have endured loss and trauma cope with their experiences. Reading tragic stories allows them to process what happened to them while maintaining distance from the painful memories and emotions' (p.121).

Through story we can allow children to explore moral dilemmas, to question choices, to understand consequences, to grapple with difficult issues and to reflect: all at a safe distance from reality. We can use metaphor to introduce ideas and to gently explore subjects without ever having to peel back the layers of protection as the child absorbs ideas and thinks in freedom. We can allow children to volunteer their thoughts and feelings, their identifications and their likes and dislikes, without questioning the validity of these ideas. This gives them a sense of autonomy and allows them the space to take from a story that which they are ready for.

We need to bear in mind that story can be presented to children in many different modalities – yes, in verbal or book form, but also in rhyme and poetry, in music or song, in movement and dance, in strokes of artwork, in the parting of sand and the forming of clay. In this way we are able to include those children who may not have the verbal or reading skills to engage on a literate level but who can access narrative in a sensorial way. As we work with children, we are able to create a story environment where stories make up the flow of engagement, where both parties dip in and out of story – of fact, fiction, fantasy and fun – with delight and with ease. As we do this, as we provide children with the modalities and vocabulary to express themselves, this in turn furnishes their minds with the necessary tools to bring healing through absorption, assimilation, creation and expression.

BIBLIOTHERAPY

We have, I'm sure, all come across stories or read books that have felt perfect for certain times in our lives; books with which we have connected on a deep level because they have reminded us that we are not isolated, that we are part of a greater human whole; books that have allowed us to process thoughts and feelings, have inspired us to persevere in spite of adversity, perhaps to hold on to something or indeed to let go. We have, perhaps, read books that have resonated deeply for others in our lives, ones we have recommended or passed on to them because we feel that the texts are able to speak deeply to their current life circumstances or struggle. This process of using books in a therapeutic form is known as bibliotherapy, which can be described as the use of stories or texts for the purpose of healing.

> A book may be able to reach where an adult cannot. (Maich and Kean 2004, p.5)

In terms of working with children, bibliotherapy can further be described as 'a child reading about a character who successfully resolves a problem similar to the one the child is experiencing' (Sullivan and Strang 2002/2003, n.p.). It is a therapy that has evolved over the years, having first been adopted in work with adult medical patients, and later used in an emotional capacity before being implemented to address the developmental needs of children (ibid.). It is considered to be a valuable process due to:

- the possibility that children may find it easier to express themselves using stories – being that stories are meaningful to them; they are familiar with the story process, and they are often comfortable with the use of metaphor and symbol (Carlson 2001, p.92)

- the belief that solving problems through literature – due to its indirect nature – could be viewed as non-invasive and, thus, child friendly (Sullivan and Strang 2002/2003)

- the belief that using stories or narratives can aid children in understanding that 'a separation exists between the self and the problem' (Carlson 2001, p.92)

- 'a belief that messages in stories could positively affect unconscious processes, even if the unconscious mind was not actively
  processing such messages' (Carlson 2001, p.92).

Margot Sunderland, in *Using Story Telling as a Therapeutic Tool with
Children* (2000), writes about how children listen to therapeutic stories.
She explains that if the story is aptly chosen, the child will

> identify with the main character in the story. In so doing, he will go on
> the same journey as the character. He will suffer the character's defeats
> and obstacles but also feel the character's courage to continue. As the
> child goes along the journey with the main character in the story, he no
> longer feels alone with his problems and his too painful or too difficult
> feelings because, hey presto! the character in the book is having them
> too. (p.17)

And the value of story used as a therapeutic tool lies in the fact that, after
hearing a very carefully considered and chosen story, the child will hold
two images of the painful situation in his mind – the pre-story (old) one
and the post-story (new) one with the new one enriched with creative
possibility from the story heard. There is sometimes a blending of the
new with the old, with the new version beginning to eclipse the old one.
The indication of the gaining of the child's attention, whereby the story
can provide a source of emotional support and instil 'images of a new
hope in his head' (Sunderland 2000, p.17), will be when the child requests
that the story be read again and again.

There is a discussion as to whether bibliotherapy should take place
only in a therapeutic context in order to avoid damage being done by
the possible selection of an inappropriate text for a child; however,
many psychologists believe that children can benefit from meaningful
material read to them by parents and practitioners. As previously
mentioned, it is a natural process, for many of us, to think of others
when we encounter certain stories in terms of the learning opportunities
they provide. Stories may not solve problems in their entirety, if at all,
but they often act as a springboard for the discussion of issues and the
resulting emotions. Sunderland (2000, p.6) says:

> Parent–child, teacher–child or counsellor–child communications about
> feelings when everyday language is used are likely to be impoverished.

The conversation will tend to lack depth and expression on both sides. It will have none of the subtleties, the complexities about felt life from a communication spoken in the realm of the imagination.

Stories, however, through the use of metaphor and fantasy, offer a far richer experience for children and can therefore provide parents and practitioners with greater insight into what a child may be thinking and/ or feeling.

Some of the other benefits of bibliotherapy for children are:

- An awareness that others have faced similar problems to the ones they or people close to them are experiencing.

- The awareness of alternative solutions to their problems through the discovery and exploration of different ideas and approaches leading to solutions-based thinking.

- The development of a liberty to discuss problems, possibly under the veil of a story or through an openness about their own life experiences encouraged by the story process. A story, when offered gently and carefully, allows children to determine their level of both exposure to the story content and their disclosure in response.

- The growth of problem-solving skills through the discovery and exploration of different ideas and approaches.

- The further development of a positive self-concept which is often due to both the content of the stories offered and the sense of agency and autonomy that is developed as the children read, assimilate the information and draw conclusions based on their experiences and emotions, with lessons learned through their choosing and at their pace.

- Relief of emotional or mental stress. I believe that part of the make-up of emotional or mental stress experienced by children (and adults) is a feeling of isolation. Once children understand the universality of the issues that affect humans, there is an element of relief that is experienced.

- The development of honesty in self-image. The process of story gives children time and space to reflect, to compare and to contrast. These processes don't end when the story does but continue in accordance with the relevance and effectiveness of the story.

- The growth of interests beyond the self. Story can be used to encourage a broader and more outward-looking focus by highlighting the struggles and triumphs of others.

- The fostering of a better understanding of human behaviour.

(Maich and Kean 2004)

Implementing bibliotherapy requires us to examine stories in terms of their content as well as considering the knowledge of the children in terms of 'literature, reading and language' (Carlson 2001). As parents and practitioners, we can read stories written by authors with a story focus; these narratives can be described as being 'true to the story' (Little 2001, p.221). When using these stories, we can allow children to draw out the relevant learning, arriving at their own conclusions. We can also choose books that have been created with specific learning objectives in mind, be they moral, spiritual, character development or knowledge focused. We do need to bear in mind that these books are more prescriptive in nature due to their explicit explanations of lessons, which somewhat lessens both the cover and the distance that story naturally creates. They may also take a kind of sacred processing space from the children. As Gray (2014) stated, implicit lessons seem to work best for children, and it is often in this space of working out a story that children develop a greater sense of ownership of the learning, then being able to apply it to their own lives.

Sunderland (2000) explains that the 'indirect expression of a therapeutic story is where both its safety and wisdom lie' (p.18). She explains that the use of story to help children with feelings is a move away from a direct focus on the child to a focus on and examination of the lives of the characters, in 'this way the child does not feel exposed in the spotlight, embarrassed, humiliated, got at or shamed. After all, it is the character in the book that is feeling X or Y, isn't it?' (p.18). Sunderland further explains that the most effective stories are the ones that are accurate in terms of addressing the pain with which the child may be grappling on both a conscious and unconscious level.

The indirect manner of the story allows for it to affect them on both levels with the message often being received on the unconscious level. She is humble in her description of an error in once creating a powerful story to use with a child who had experienced much trauma in her life. The little girl was totally engrossed as Sunderland used metaphors to symbolize the abuse and cruelty that this child had experienced, but in the end she made the mistake of using the little girl's own name to name the child in the story, causing her to rush out of the room. Sunderland (2000) recounts, 'I had blown her cover, and taken her into the realm of shame and exposure' (p.19). A story that blatantly addresses a child's issues with 'no indirectness via metaphor, images and character', she explains, 'is an attack on a child's dignity' (p.19), and simply reports the child's situation, often loaded with judgement. The power of the therapeutic story lies in its indirect expression.

Other aspects to think about when choosing books in a therapeutic context include:

- Clarity – Is the story simple, brief and easy to grasp?

- Is the story either feasible or fantastical enough to capture and hold the children's interest?

- Relevance – Does the story fit with relevant issues, feelings, needs, interests and goals?

- Respectability – Does the story demonstrate healthy values and respect for others through cultural diversity, gender inclusivity and acceptance?

- Hopeful – Do the characters demonstrate coping skills and resilience, and does the problem situation show resolution?

(Adapted from Carlson 2001; Cartledge and Kiarie 2001)

TEACHERS AS AGENTS OF HEALING

The stories we choose can be effective, not only on an individual but also on a group level, fostering healing and reconciliation, and establishing peace, with teachers often possessing the capacity to facilitate these processes. As the UNICEF report *The Role of Teachers in Peacebuilding*

(Horner *et al.* 2015) says, teachers may at times 'act as agents of healing and...play a significant part in peacebuilding.' The concept of peace education is derived from peace studies and is defined by UNICEF as:

> The process of promoting the knowledge, skills, attitudes and values needed to bring about behaviour changes that will enable children, youth and adults to prevent conflict and violence, both overt and structural; to resolve conflict peacefully; and to create the conditions conducive to peace, whether at an intrapersonal, interpersonal, intergroup, national or international level. (Fountain 1999, p.1)

This type of education is implemented through both content and pedagogy. Content would require inclusivity, justice and fairness: for example ensuring that all groups in a community or nation are represented equally, while pedagogy would include encouraging skills like critical thinking, collaboration, problem solving, etc. around the storywork.

I would propose that story in all its forms would serve as the most natural and effective resource in imparting peace-fortifying values. And it is indeed essential to promote training and resources that cover multiple perspectives, specifically in areas of conflict, as there are, unfortunately, as verified by the report, 'examples of teachers manipulating nation building aspects of the curriculum such as History or Geography to represent their own biases and views of history, constructing allies and enemies from their own perspective and re/producing national narratives' (Horner *et al.* 2015, p.22).

If we, as parents and practitioners, do not expose children to the stories and journeys of all peoples, considering their journeys with empathy and compassion, then I would suggest that we are leaving unfulfilled the call to act as agents of peace in the lives of our children. However, it is not only the exposure to stories and the reading of books that provides healing. The narrative process, and the creation of story in all its many forms, while a gift to and for others, can also be a gift of healing to the creators themselves.

As George Dawes Green of The Moth said, the storytelling process allows storytellers to connect events in their own lives, to gain insight into them and to learn new lessons as they weave them together in newly constructed formats. And this process of revisiting one's life's stories can improve mental, spiritual and emotional well-being and physical health, again demonstrating how story affects us on many different levels, both as we receive it and as we express it.

THE WHOLE-BODY EFFECT OF STORY

In 1968, Professor James Pennebaker at the University of Texas in Austin carried out a study exploring the power of language in relieving trauma. He began by asking his students to identify personal experiences that they had found to be highly stressful or traumatic.

> He then divided the class into three groups: One would write about what was currently going on in their lives; the second would write about the details of the traumatic or stressful event; and the third would recount the facts of the experience, their feelings and emotions about it, and what impact they thought this event had had on their lives. All of the students wrote continuously for fifteen minutes on four consecutive days whilst sitting alone. (van der Kolk 2015b, p.239)

It was reported that the students responded to the task set in earnest, with many disclosing previously unrevealed secrets. A frequent topic of writing was the death of a family member, and out of a total of 200 students, 65 wrote about childhood trauma, with 22 per cent of the women and 10 per cent of the men in the study writing about sexual trauma experienced prior to the age of 17. The researchers also studied the health of the students and found a correlation between the trauma experienced and their number of hospital visits, with the students who reported a traumatic sexual experience in childhood having been hospitalized an average of 1.7 days in the previous year, almost twice the rate of the other students in the study. The team then considered the number of health centre visits prior to the study and in the month afterwards. The results showed that the students who had written both about their trauma and their emotional response had a 50 per cent drop in doctor visits compared to the other two groups. Their writing had led to improvements in their mood, outlook and physical health.

In a subsequent study Pennebaker worked with a group of 72 students. He asked half of them to speak about the most traumatic experience in their lives and the other half to speak about their plans for the day. As the students spoke, their blood pressure, heart rate, muscle tension and hand temperature were measured. The study showed clear results in both the short and long term. The students who felt and expressed their emotions initially experienced a change in all of their physiological reactions with increases across the board. Astonishingly however, afterwards, their arousal levels 'fell to levels below where they had been at the start of the study. The decrease in blood pressure could still be measured six weeks after the experiment ended' (van der Kolk 2015b, p.240).

But what do these studies speak to in terms of children? Esfahani Smith (2017, p.174) says that, in Pennebaker's research, 'the subjects who benefitted the most after the experiment were those who demonstrated the greatest progress in sense-making over time. These were people whose initial responses were emotionally raw and their stories disjointed, but whose narratives became smoother and more insightful as each day passed.' Pennebaker, in fact, found that the process of writing was uniquely healing in that it 'allows people to systematically process an event, bringing order to it', that 'through writing' people 'discover new insights and come to understand how the crisis fits into the broader mosaic of their lives' (Esfahani Smith 2017, p.175).

I would propose that as children have not yet developed the sophisticated language of adults, it is play that serves the same purpose for them that writing does for adults. It is the playing-out of experiences that is transformative for their well-being on every level. The child, in play, even with limited language skills, is able to sort through, analyse and integrate their experiences. This imaginative play can inhabit any number of modalities – miming, dancing, drawing, crafting – and it acts as a precursor to more sophisticated language and to script. And it is sometimes carried out alone, or often in collaboration with both the adults closest to the child and/or with their peers.

As children develop further, it is the crafting and retelling of stories that provides a way in which they can begin to make sense of them on an emotional level. This creation and retelling can take many forms – drawing, acting, playing, crafting, dancing – all acting as a precursor to script. And they do this in collaboration with both the adults closest to them and, often, their peers. In studies of Baltimore families talking about the past, Peggy Miller showed that children often describe upsetting experiences to their parents with the stories expressed creating two levels of emotional transaction: a replay of whatever they went through and the emotional response they elicit upon telling the story (Miller *et al.* 1992). As they tell the story, it affords them time to think about the story content, to evaluate their feelings and to gain further perspective based on the responses they receive. Bruner (1986, n.p.) suggests that the adult's reaction is crucially important in the retelling process as it has the potential to be 'vivid enough to make the retelling cathartic, and at the same time calm enough to make the retelling safe and helpful'. He also proposes that children benefit from the distance the retelling of a story provides, with the narrative acting as a 'cooling vessel' (Engel 2016, p.10) in which emotionally and cognitively powerful experiences can be reconstructed with less impact than they originally had. Again, we see how respectful adult engagement can allow for children's processing of experience. Children may not be able to write in order to make sense of the events of their lives, but parents and practitioners can provide outlets of expression for them, ones that will generate the same healing benefits that the writing process and inherent sense-making generates for adults.

SOCIETAL HEALING

It is evident that story can provide healing for people on an individual level. We are able to be healed as we take stories in, and there is potential for healing through the composition and expression of stories. But story does not only function on an individual level, it is also evident on a collective, societal level.

As mentioned previously, stories can be used both for evil and for good, to destroy and to build. The author Chimamanda Ngozi Adichie (2009) says 'Stories have been used to dispossess and to malign. But stories can also be used to empower, and to humanize. Stories can break the dignity of a people. But stories can also repair that broken dignity.' I recently read factual accounts of some of the many victims of the apartheid regime in South Africa in a book titled *All That Was Lost* (Byrne 2010). The book simply notes their stories, word for word, as they were spoken to the interviewer. These victims had been invited to give their accounts to the Truth and Reconciliation Commission (TRC), which was created after the collapse of the apartheid system, in order to 'establish the truth about the past, grant amnesty where appropriate and establish measures for reparation' (*TRC Report*, Vol. 1, Ch. 2, Sec. 3, cited by Byrne 2010, p.vii). Many of the victims who had told their stories expressed their sense of frustration that no action had been taken as a result of their testimony, and remained frustrated, with their struggle seemingly ongoing and their suffering unresolved. I was moved to investigate the subject further and was interested to find research carried out on storytelling and its role in the process of reconciliation.

In the paper 'Shattered Stories: Healing and Reconciliation in the South African Context', Cori Wielenga (2013) discusses John Paul Lederach's four-part model for reconciliation, a model that 'encompasses mercy, truth, justice and peace', with these elements 'most significantly enacted through storytelling' (p.1). Wielenga quotes Lederach, who describes storytelling as 'a living, interactive process through which new ways of engaging and being with one another are born'. We indeed know that storytelling is an interactive process and that stories can bring about holistic change on an individual level. But how, as Lederach says, can stories lead to new ways of being with one another? And why then the frustration of the TRC witnesses who experienced and expressed their disappointment with the storytelling process? Why did their painful accounts not lead to some sense of resolution? Along with ongoing socio-economic struggles unsolved through lack of reparations, lasting physical pain from injuries inflicted, the effects of trauma and grief, we can also possibly find an answer in Wielanga's paper where he looks to Anthony Balcomb (2000, n.p.), who says that 'sharing stories has the biggest impact when we allow our story to be shattered and transformed by that of the other. This includes the shattering of stereotypes, assumptions and ideas that sustain the divisions between us.'

It could be argued that, perhaps due to a percentage of white South Africans failing to engage with the TRC and with the stories being shared by the victims, those victims were left feeling unheard and resentful (Hamber, Nageng and O'Malley 2000), with the disengaged white South Africans unaffected by the accounts of the storytellers and unchanged as a result. Wielanga suggests that the need in these situations of injustice 'is not for perpetrators to be punished or for financial compensation as much as it is for the perceived perpetrators to engage in victims' stories' (p.4). In all societies there is a need for everyone's stories to be deemed equally important, and to be equally acknowledged. We otherwise risk the alienation of peoples from each other. From just this one societal example we again witness the remarkable need for human beings to craft and to tell their individual stories and to be heard by those around them

The story process requires imagination. If we can imagine the life of another and empathise with them, only then can we begin to feel compassion and be moved to change our ideas and confront our prejudices, and if necessary to take action to help in some way. The stories of others and our individual stories are not formed in isolation. We form part of families, communities and societies and we are affected by each other on every level. 'Not only are our personal life stories embedded in the stories of others, but they are also embedded in the contending narratives of the past and current social, cultural and political narratives' (Cobley 2001, p.2). As we view life through a story lens, and begin to 'enlarge the range' (Wielanga 2013, p.2) of our personal story to include the stories of others – and be moved by them – we become more able to reflect on our own stories and how they are lived out, and to critique them. This shattering, moving and self-reflection leads to the creation of new individual and collective stories.

As we engage in and with the stories of each other:

- Human dignity is restored.

- People feel validated in themselves, and in relationship with each other.

- Differences are accepted, and sometimes celebrated.

- The boundaries between groups are renegotiated, leading to a point of shared identity beyond the boundary.

- Understanding is fostered.

- Peaceful co-existence becomes possible.

(Wielanga 2013, p.6)

If we can start, from a very young age, to introduce children to the stories of others and to communicate what life may look like for other children (and people) in their communities and further afield, then we will have created an awareness that their life stories are not created in isolation but indeed include the life stories of others. In light of this, we can consider what stories we choose to tell to children.

WHAT STORIES DO WE CHOOSE TO TELL?

It's not merely the ability to read that matters. It's how and what and why we read.

Sue Palmer (n.d.)

There are many different stories to choose from and, as caregivers and practitioners, we need to be intentional as we make our choices. Stories that may seem frivolous can often impart joy, and those that seem intense or dark can, as we have seen, allow people to process complex issues and provide space for healing. Stories that allow children to gain an insight into the lives of others develop their empathy, and those that depict heroic acts can inspire courage and resilience.

When considering the stories that we tell children, we can consider the following questions:

- Does the story include a variety of voices? We can consider race, ethnicity, class, ability, religion, age, immigration status and/ or socio-economic status. And does it promote equality and inclusion?

- Does the story misrepresent people in any way or perpetuate negative stereotypes? Or does it promote justice, developing an awareness of prejudice or injustice?

- Does the story promote action, developing the virtues of kindness and compassion, encouraging an awareness of rights and responsibilities, along with the ability to speak out against injustice and resolve conflicts?

- Does the story promote peace, developing the desire to live in peace with others?

We can also carefully consider the language of the stories we tell. Stories contain rich language: 'Vygotsky argued that language reflects our culture and its forms, whether in academic texts, professional practice, the arts, folklore or customs' (Smith *et al.* 2003, p.500). He also proposed that children become thinkers and learners according to speech that is heard and used in social interactions. They then construct monologues of their own, which initially are used to communicate with others but later act as 'a form of communication with the self' (Smith *et al.* 2003, p.500) – a kind of inner speech, as a tool of self-regulation and as thought (p.501).

It is both the content and the language of stories that will assist children in developing personal narratives that are understanding and compassionate to themselves and to others. Through the use of story we can help children to create an internal voice that is kind. Of course, not every story will meet all of the above criteria, and indeed some stories may focus in more detail on one aspect as opposed to others. But by generally considering stories in the light of the above criteria, and by asking the question 'What will the children's personal narrative, aided by their internal thought processes, sound like?', we can begin to create more just and peaceful communities.

Chapter 6

Story and Metaphor

KANELLA BOUKOUVALA

Since the birth of the human species, people have communicated with each other to share information, experiences and needs and to inform one another about possible danger and threats to their survival.

In his book *The Irresistible Fairy Tale: The Cultural and Social History of a Genre* (2013), Jack Zipes states that humans have potentially been telling stories before we even had the ability to speak, using forms of sign language to communicate. Today we have visual representations of such stories in the form of ancient cave paintings, such as the ones in Altamira Cave in Spain, that possibly depict artistic scenes of hunting and everyday life.

We do not know exactly when verbal communication and written language were born but we do have some clues. Until recently it was believed that texts of ancient wisdom in Sumerian from around the third millennium BC were the oldest texts in the world. Recent findings in Greece point to the existence of written language possibly predating this. Texts, poems, songs, myths and religious ideas in story form have been discovered in all ancient cultures showing that storytelling is fundamental in human nature and has always been deemed to be necessary.

Why are stories so important to us? As previously mentioned, and as Frank Rose says in *The Art of Immersion* (2011), stories are composed in patterns that are recognizable to us, and all expressions of story have something in common. This is what Jung terms archetype: a character, a pattern or a symbol that represents a form of energy in the human psyche. It is due to these universal archetypes that tales, stories and myths from across the globe have many similarities despite the fact that they were developed in different cultures. Even though many of them were passed down through the ages from the mouths of different storytellers, taking many different forms or scripts, the ones that prevailed are those that the people chose to be consistent and in keeping with the original archetypes (Low *et al.* 2010).

Stories, as we read in Burns' book *101 Healing Stories for Kids and Teens* (2005, p.3), inform, educate, teach values and discipline, build experience, facilitate problem solving, promote challenge and heal.

They possess 'many important characteristics of effective comm- unication' in that they are attractive and therefore effective teaching tools, bypassing resistance, lending themselves to interaction, nurturing imagination, creating outcome possibilities and inviting independent decision making. Through stories one is often able to 'see' the unseen, the invisible: the abstract meanings that cannot be grasped with the senses. And all of these stories, legends, myths and fables can be used with both children and adults, and they can aid in healing, encourage changes in behaviour, the navigation of relationships (through the presentation of different, sometimes new perspectives and the exploration of moral choices) and the regulation of emotions and emotional arousal (Fox Eades 2006).

At the same time, shared stories facilitate attachment (Burns 2005), enhance the bonding process and establish relationships, for example when grandparents tell stories and fairy tales to their grandchildren.

Of course, when using stories, the voice of the storyteller is of prime importance. The storyteller's voice through tone, pitch, musicality and pauses can have a great effect that makes all the difference. Another essential aspect is the use of humour and prompts, used during or after the sharing of a story. Items such as toys, puppets, dolls or other objects such as musical instruments can be used (items which aim to activate all five senses as the listener listens to the story).

Stories, especially fairy tales, often contain themes of abuse, neglect and trauma, even in immediate families. Think, for example, of Cinderella. There are also issues of bereavement, bullying and sibling rivalry. Texts like the Bible, the Quran and others are full of stories about people living together in harmony, but many holy books also contain stories of violence and war. The stories that many of us are familiar with, that form a part of our culture, are about both good and evil, about justice and injustice. There are many kinds of stories that we are exposed to throughout the course of our lives and all of them help us to understand ourselves and to make choices.

Not all stories include a fiction character. Stories can also be simple narratives about everyday life, and even these can be powerful in bringing about desired outcomes.

A few years ago I had to write a bedtime story for a boy who was 10 years old. He was unable to sleep in his bed alone, getting up at night to visit his parents' or brother's bed. After discussing the science of sleep with his parents and giving them all the necessary information about a good sleep, I wrote a story for the boy in book form with illustrations and his own picture in it. The story described, using words and pictures, the routines that the boy and his parents would follow before and after going to bed, giving clues about when it was time to get up. Of course, I had to write a similar bedtime storybook for his brother as well! The result was that the boy never experienced problems with getting up in the night again but rather stayed in his bed at night, having a full night's sleep. As he said to his parents, having his bedtime story next to him made him feel safe.

Life stories can be a powerful tool, bringing healing and connection to a family who are struggling with difficult and complex issues. The use of story can help a child to regulate emotions and to change their internal working model towards a more positive and healthier one. Life stories have the potential to literally change lives.

Another client of mine was a cancer survivor. When her younger son was 2 years old and her eldest 6, she was diagnosed with stage-three thyroid cancer. Although thyroid cancer has one of the best prognoses, she experienced difficulties during her treatment, and a year later she heard from her doctor that they felt that the treatment was not proceeding 'well'. Indeed, since the first moment she heard the word 'cancer', fear had nested in her heart: the fear of not seeing her children grow up, and the fear that they would not remember her after she died because they were very young.

In the end my client overcame all of her medical difficulties and did well. However, her younger son on entering primary school was diagnosed with a learning difficulty which was described as 'emotional immaturity'. His symptoms presented in terms of writing and learning. His writing was illegible, and he avoided studying even though he was very clever. When required to write a complex word, he would write the first and the last syllable of the word, skipping the middle, but would read it as a whole word. He would become very upset when his mother tried to explain his errors to him. His poor academic performance continued to be a problem. When examined again in the first year of high school, it was then that his therapist discovered that his mother was a cancer survivor. She instructed the mother to begin to talk to her sons about her illness and her fears and difficulties during that time.

My client, following the therapist's suggestion, decided to speak to her sons during the approaching Christmas holidays. They sat together as a family around the fireplace and she began to tell them about her cancer diagnosis, the treatments she had undergone and her decision to leave them with their grandmother for two months due to the fact that her treatment included radioactive iodine, and their young age at the time, leaving her with no other option. She also spoke to them honestly about her fears, and the fact that she had no way to communicate those fears to them, thinking that they could not fully understand because of their age, and trying to protect them from their own fears of losing their mother. They ended up hugging and crying together. The day that school started after the Christmas holidays, her younger son came running towards her as school ended, yelling, 'Mum, can you see? Can you see?', showing her his notebook. His writing was as clear as if it had been printed. He was so surprised! They were all so surprised! His learning difficulties had vanished. Soon afterwards, he became one of the best students in his class and proceeded to university, skipping the master's degree stage and being offered a place to proceed directly to his PhD studies.

My client's life story, when communicated clearly to her son, helped him to gain insight into his own self, better understand his own experience, untangle his emotions and finally flourish and thrive, fulfilling his full potential.

We often find a plethora of metaphors in stories, myths, legends, parables, etc. We can call these small units, objects or phrases 'symbols'. For example, when my own son was young and wanted to express his concern about me and my feelings to his grandmother on a particular day, he would say 'My mum is wearing lipstick today'. Lipstick had become a symbol for my bad mood to him. And it was true. When I was feeling down and wanted to cheer up a bit, I used to wear lipstick.

Much has been written about metaphors and their use and value in terms of personal development and healing. People in ancient times knew how powerful metaphors could be, with Aesop's Fables and the parables we find in the Bible just a few examples of this. We may be unaware of it but in everyday life we constantly talk in metaphors. We say things like, 'I'm drowning in this case', meaning we have a lot of work, or 'I'm as hungry as a wolf', 'I have ghosts in my closet', or 'It's raining cats and dogs'. Metaphors are powerful when used correctly, as they convey a sometimes abstract idea simply using a picture to create meaning. Just as for Jung, dreams act as the royal avenue towards the unconscious, so for Mills and Crowley (1986) metaphors are the key to opening and activating the 'right brain' and gaining access to the realm of emotions, fantasy and creativity.

But why use metaphors? After all, there is nothing wrong with using plain language in trying to convey what one means. Well, experience shows us that the results are just not the same when using language as when using a metaphor. As the saying goes, 'A picture is worth a thousand words.'

Stories have been used in the work of the master of hypnosis Milton Erickson. In hypnosis, a therapist after capturing the client's attention, directs it inwards. It is here, in a trance state, that the client can grasp the meaning of stories, dreams, symbols and other unconscious experiences. If this 'unconscious learning' is not against the client's moral principles and values, then there may be a change in the state of mind of the client that opens the pathway towards improved mental health. Through this pathway, one could use stories or even simple conversations with the use of indirect, interspersed suggestions to impose a kind of restorative learning on an unconscious level to the client (Erikson, Rossi and Rossi 1976).

Joyce Mills suggests that the use of metaphors can bring change, increase resilience and heal, both in children and adults. A beautiful metaphor in her training and work is one known as the 'Butterfly Cycle' (Mills and Crowley 2014). I used this with a suicidal adolescent I was working with.

The adolescent was a girl of 17 years of age who was flirting with the idea of suicide. Her mother, a single parent, was busy trying to cope with life's difficulties. She had not been able to apply firm and consistent boundaries with her daughter. The girl's father was not always present in her life as he was dealing with his own demons in a remote village in Greece. This led to her feelings of loneliness and abandonment. She was about to finish high school and had no idea as to what she wanted to do with her life.

One day, as she was telling me what had happened during the last week, I commented, 'As I am listening to you, I do not know why, but a story came to my mind. A story about a beautiful butterfly. Do you know that when the butterfly comes to a certain age, she finds a safe place, a safe leaf and it is there that she lays her eggs? The eggs are safe there, hidden from birds and insects by other leaves. Soon afterwards, under the right conditions, the eggs hatch and small caterpillars come out of the eggs. They start eating immediately. There is enough food around, there is the leaf on which the eggs were laid, the surrounding leaves… And when they come to a point where they have grown up to five times in size, then the caterpillars are ready to go and find a special place on the tree to create their nest, their cocoon. Slowly, they start producing the material and build their cocoon. As soon as they finish it, they get in and the cocooning phase begins. Did you know that during this phase the caterpillar turns into a soupy material inside the cocoon? Yes, it does! And yet the caterpillar carries within it certain cells called "imaginal discs" that *carry the full information for and potential of a butterfly*. Then, when it is ready, the caterpillar, through this soupy mess, transforms into a beautiful butterfly inside the cocoon. But even if you are able to see the fully shaped, beautiful butterfly under the now transparent wall of the cocoon, if one tries to free it by opening the cocoon, the butterfly will not survive. The butterfly needs to stretch her legs and body, in order to strengthen it, before she is ready to break her own cocoon. Then the butterfly is ready to come out. And yet, she is not yet ready to fly. This beautiful creature, coming out to freedom, is not yet ready. If one tries to push her to fly, she will die. First, she needs to dry her wings thoroughly before she is ready to master flying. So many stages…so many transformations…order…chaos…beauty…'

The girl stayed silent for a while, exhibiting no sign of any emotion. She was looking down. And suddenly she said, 'You know what? I am like the butterfly. I am in my own darkness. I am a mess, and I need time to find those cells you told me about, the ones that carry the full potential. Then I need time to transform into who I want to be. And I know I will. I just need to find what it is I want.' We never mentioned the butterfly story again. Though, since that day, the girl started wanting to work to find out what her potential was. Using another metaphor, I suggested that she create a collage by looking deeply into her heart and trying to find what *'the things that made her heart sing'* were. Never again did she venture to the roof to try to jump, and she rarely had visits of the *'darkness'*, as she called her dark heavy thoughts.

Many types of metaphors are used when talking to children, and they are just as powerful when used with adults. The girl that waits for her prince on a beautiful white horse, the frog that turns into a prince with just one kiss, the ugly duckling that turns into a beautiful swan, and so many other characters that live happily ever after!

According to Barker (1996) there are many types of metaphors, but we can divide them into eight major categories consisting of major stories, anecdotes and short stories, analogies, similes and brief metaphorical statements, relationship metaphors, tasks and rituals, metaphorical objects, artistic metaphors, and cartoon therapy. I would also add living metaphors from the work of Mills and Crowley (2014) to this list.

I would say that one needs to be familiar with these metaphors and be able to use them properly if they are to be used in therapy. This can look deceivingly easy at times but both proper training and skill are required in order to achieve therapeutic results using metaphors.

A student of mine, for her therapeutic story assignment, created a story for a young child of 9 years of age who had two siblings: a sister of 12 years of age, and a brother of 5 years. Her issue was sibling rivalry, as she felt that she could not find her place in her family due to the fact that she was always in the middle and could not enjoy the benefits of being the oldest or the youngest child. She complained that her parents would say things like:

'The two older ones…help your mother with groceries.'

'The two younger ones…it's time to go to bed.'

So the therapist wrote a story, about a ship with three sails. A big one, a medium one and a small one. The medium sail was the one that was the most used. And on occasion, when the sea became rough, the small and the big one proved to be very useful, and helped the middle one to do its job the best way. But all three of them were equally valuable. After listening to the story, the girl said nothing; however, in the review session that followed, the parents reported that there was no longer sibling rivalry between their children, and that the girl had drawn a boat with three sails and hung it on the wall in their living room.

Many times in my own work with clients I have used an activity proposed by Mills and Crowley (2014), with both children and adults, which has been adapted here.

Whatever the feelings or thoughts that are currently bothering my client, if I find it appropriate, I recommend that they design how they feel with 'colour, line and shape' on an A4 piece of paper. Then, on a second piece of paper, I ask them to design with 'colour, line and shape' what it would look like if it was all better. After that, I ask them to look closely at what they designed on paper 1 and paper 2, and on a third paper I invite them to design with 'colour, line and shape' what it takes to go from paper 1 to paper 2.

The results of this activity, however immature the drawings, never cease to amaze me. It is not what people draw on the third paper. It is the internal process of a possible resolution that arises in them and, as if by magic, it takes away almost all the distress from their feelings and thoughts. One can witness the change in them soon after the session. Many times they do not connect the change with the three drawings as the change happens on an unconscious level.

In literature we find a lot of stories using metaphors with multiple meanings. As adults and children engage with the story, they can choose the meaning that resonates with their own hearts, their inner selves.

Have you ever witnessed a child listening to a story told by their mother during bedtime or by a grandparent as they sit on his/her lap? If you have, you have almost certainly noticed how engaged the child is, how relaxed – almost trance-like, and yet simultaneously alert – so much so that if the story is familiar to them, they will immediately protest should the story go off course. From research we know that when a person is listening to a story containing metaphors, the brain lights up in a way that can be described as a 'Christmas tree'.

The book *Touching Clay: Touching What?* (Souter-Anderson 2010, p.75) mentions 'that metaphor lights up multiple centres in the brain enabling increased connectivity'. This 'firing together' is what causes wiring together, as neurobiology scientists like Daniel Siegel tell us. And this firing and wiring through metaphors is what sculpts the brain in a positive, new way and gives new meaning to a person's experience, opening the pathway to healing trauma and painful wounds in the psyche, and aiding them in learning how to be in the world and how to relate to others.

As MacIntyre (1981) says, 'the narrative of any one life is part of an interlocking set of narratives' and people will only know what they are to do when they begin to understand what stories they are a part of, how others respond to them and how their responses to others should be construed in turn. Stories not only provide healing for past experiences, they continually model possibilities for different ways of being and knowing.

> Deprive children of stories and you leave them unscripted, anxious stutterers in their actions as in their words... Mythology, in its original sense, is at the heart of things. (MacIntyre 1981, p.218)

And it moves to being in the minds and hearts of people. This is the power of metaphor and the wonder of story.

Chapter 7

Diversity and Representation in Story

The story of any one of us is in some measure the story of us all.

Frederick Buechner (2019)

The world is large, and with the billions of people now inhabiting the planet it is an impossibility to explore and to understand the many lives lived. As we have discussed, story opens a door to the experiences of others and as we enter in, we become witnesses to a broad spectrum of lives lived. In fact, it is often only through access to the words and worlds of others that one will gain an insight into different human journeys, and a deeper insight into their own.

This chapter highlights a few of the ways in which we can begin to consider diversity, and some of the approaches and resources being developed and used in order to address access to story. Providing every child with access to story is urgent, as is supporting every child voicing their story. Indeed, both of these factors will have an effect on the child's well-being on every level.

As we involve children in the story process, it's essential that we present the full spectrum of humanity to them, including a representation of each child in so far as possible. Farrah Serrouk, in an article titled 'Young Children Need Stories in Which They Can Recognise Their Own Lives' (2017), suggests that one way this can be done is by asking whether the stories we're using explore themes that are at the forefront of children's minds. Examples include 'Can't You Sleep Little Bear?' by Martin Waddell, which addresses fear of the dark, and 'Strictly

No Elephants' by Lisa Mantchev, which addresses exclusion. Serrouk explains the power of representation:

> To find a fragment of yourself in the pages of a book is a profound and powerful experience; it holds a mirror up to your existence and suggests that you're not alone. For children in their formative years this is life-affirming. We have a responsibility to ensure that children experience books that reflect, value and validate their own realities.

Indeed, there are many instances we hear about in which people who are not widely represented in mainstream culture clearly remember the first time they saw someone who resembled them, and the powerful effect this had on them. In the documentary series *Shine On*, directed by Reese Witherspoon, the actress America Ferrara, an American born to parents from Honduras, discusses the lack of visibility of Latina actors in her youth and explains how important she felt it was for people to see people similar to them represented on screen in order for them to recognize themselves. She discusses her career with Witherspoon, saying what a groundbreaking opportunity it was to represent people who at the time were largely underrepresented in mainstream culture, and that this was a motivating factor in her choice of roles. Nigerian author Chimamanda Ngozi Adichie, in her 2009 TED talk titled 'The Danger of a Single Story', talks about her exposure to foreign books with foreign characters with whom she could not identify. This led her to believe that it was necessary for all books to have a kind of foreignness about them. She reflects on how much her perception of books changed when she discovered African titles (which were far more difficult to find), and how she realized that people like her could also exist in literature. She reports that this realization led to her starting to write about things that she actually recognized (le Roux 2017).

Matt de la Peña, Newbery Medal-winning author of the books *Last Stop on Market Street* and the more recent *Love*, in a January 2018 article 'Why We Shouldn't Shield Children from Darkness', discusses another aspect of diversity. He talks about the process of writing the book *Love* and issues around one particular image created for the book. He explains that, as the book was in process, he and the illustrator Loren Long learned that a major gatekeeper wouldn't support the project, which they describe as an 'exploration of love in a child's life', unless they softened the aforementioned image, one that depicts a despondent young boy hiding beneath a piano with his dog as his parents argue across the living room.

The publishers expressed concern that the moment was 'a little too heavy for children'. This caused de la Peña to re-examine his early drafts of the work, realizing, as he did so, that without the image concerned the drafts just did not ring true. Although the drafts were uplifting and reassuring, he felt that they failed to 'acknowledge any notion of adversity' and therefore failed to represent 'an uncomfortable number of children out there right now…crouched beneath a metaphorical piano' (de la Peña 2018). As de la Peña says, the book world is beginning to consider racial inclusion – and witnessing change in this area – but there are many other facets of diversity 'that remain in the shadows' (2018). For children who have experienced, and do experience, these types of circumstances, or indeed any type of adversity, how very reassuring it might be to see it acknowledged. For those children who haven't experienced adversity and are initially encountering it in difficult images, as de la Peña says, 'I can't think of a safer place to explore complex emotions for the first time than inside the pages of a book, while sitting in the lap of a loved one' (2018).

It is vitally important to recognize oneself in literature. At the same time, the representation of all people involves children witnessing lives that can differ entirely from their own, and we do not need to ensure that they are presented with only those lives and situations that are similar to theirs.

The British columnist Bel Mooney discusses the gift of reading to children and the stories she loved as a child:

> Books gave instant access to friends within other worlds. A city child, living in a council flat and at a large primary school, I had an unlikely passion for girls' boarding school stories (all prefects and pillow fights) as well as classics such as *The Secret Garden* by Frances Hodgson Burnett. What was a manor house? It didn't matter that the story was remote from my own experience. After all, that's partly the point, isn't it? I want to remind some right-on children's writers and publishers nowadays that children in council flats don't actually need to read about children in council flats. (Mooney 2018)

Borba (2016, p.78) writes:

> Books can be portals to understanding other worlds and other views, to helping our children be more open to differences and cultivate new perspectives.

Serrouk (2017) writes about the need for a school's books to reflect the reality of the worlds belonging to other people. She reminds us that stories about others allow us to 'grapple with dilemmas and perspectives outside our own frame of reference' (Serrouk 2017). Gray (2014) explains that through these processes – this understanding, this grappling – we may learn to care about people whom we might not otherwise care so much about, including people who are quite different from ourselves.

It is, indeed, our responsibility to present children with stories that are both familiar and remote, that seem plausible and within the realm of possibility, and that are impossible and fantastical and far beyond reach. *What is of paramount importance is that we present all manner of people to children in an equally positive way.* Historically there is a marked lack of diversity in the literature available to young children, and an effort is now being made to redress the balance, with this issue considered to be important and urgent. But it is not simply the representation of various groups of people that redresses the lack of diversity in children's literature. In order to truly offer a different story experience to children we need to ensure that diverse people in diverse groups are represented as standard practice. As Serrouk (2017) says:

> In our efforts to increase visibility, we must ensure we don't limit ourselves to a narrow set of representations. The representation of any community must be as diverse as the community itself. If, for example, the only books that feature ethnic minority characters in our classrooms are books in which overcoming struggle or celebrating difference are at the heart of the narrative, this can undermine the normalization of reader realities and potentially problematise self-perception. Children must never feel that they're excluded from the literary space or only entitled to restricted access.

We also need to consider the access of all children to the predominant literature of their schooling, ensuring that, as we do so, we are respecting their cultures by making story learning relevant and interesting, and acknowledging the story wisdom they bring to their learning.

Another aspect of diversity to consider is the cultural content of the stories children are exposed to and read. When we examine the focus of different cultures, we can begin to ensure that we read more widely in order to include a variety of lessons for the children.

ADDRESSING PREJUDICE

As I was researching for the purposes of this book, I was amazed to find that children generally develop their perspectives on aspects of identity such as gender and race before the age of 5. According to three separate studies carried out by York University's Faculty of Health with more than 350 white children aged between 5 and 12, with the stated goal of gaining a better understanding of the automatic racial attitudes of children, the children participating exhibited 'an implicit pro-White bias when exposed to images of both White and Black children' (York University 2017). In the study, children were asked to sort faces according to race on the category-based Implicit Association Test, with both the younger children (aged between 5 and 8) and the older children (aged between 9 and 12) displaying 'greater automatic positivity toward white as opposed to black children'. An interesting takeaway from the tests was that while children showed a positive attitude to white children they did not show a negative attitude towards black children. Professor Jennifer Steele, who conducted the research, explains, 'In early childhood what we know is that children tend to be egocentric and socio-centric. They think that they're great and that other people who are like them are great too. That's why we recommend using interventions that don't challenge these beliefs, but instead promote the fact that people from different backgrounds or who look different than them often have a lot in common and they can be great too' (York University 2017). Exposure to a wide range of stories can begin to represent this array of greatness to children.

In a 2014 article in the *Journal of Applied Psychology*, a study into reducing prejudice among children detailed how it set out to show that 'extended contact via story reading is a powerful strategy to improve out-group attitudes' (Vezzali *et al.* 2015, p.105). The authors conducted three different studies to test whether reading the Harry Potter series improved attitudes towards stigmatized groups, for example refugees and immigrants. The reason for choosing the series was due to its seemingly universal appeal and its focus on intergroup topics (with these groups being fantastical and not representative of any real group of people). The studies, which involved one experimental intervention with elementary school children and two cross-sectional studies with high school and university students in both Italy and the United Kingdom, supported the main hypothesis and indicated 'identification with the main character (i.e. Harry Potter), disidentification from the negative character (i.e. Voldemort) and the emergence of perspective taking which resulted in attitude improvement'.

The authors of the same paper also cited interesting findings by Cameron and colleagues (Cameron and Rutland 2006; Cameron *et al.* 2006, 2011) who conducted a series of studies where English children aged between 5 and 11 years of age read short stories of friendship between in-group and out-group characters. It was found that exposure to the stories resulted in improved attitudes towards various often-stigmatized groups such as refugees and disabled people. However, what is further discussed is that many of the studies that explore these in-out-group dynamics often use stories that are created specifically for the purposes of the study. The authors argue that books created – and indeed published – with the explicit purpose of addressing 'cross-group friendships may be limited due to (a) their specific focus and context and (b) the (perhaps limited) appeal they have to readers'. They also argue that 'such stories are likely to see improved attitudes only toward the target group involved in the stories themselves'.

So what, you may ask, is the answer in terms of sourcing relevant and appropriate materials? The authors here suggest the use of fantasy works already published due both to their appeal and to the fact that, as mentioned previously, the stigmatized characters are not representative of any real-life people. This allows for generalization and also allows for individuals to make the associations themselves – either as someone who may be prejudicial in their thinking towards others or as someone who may be experiencing prejudice.

Another fascinating aspect of the study is that the stated hypothesis is in line with two theories. The first is known as parasocial contact hypothesis (Schiappa, Gregg and Hewes 2005) which suggests that 'cognitive and affective responses following exposure to media characters are similar to those produced by direct contact experiences' (Vezzali *et al.* 2015, p.106). The second is social cognitive theory (Bandura 1997, 2002) which proposes that through the process of abstract modelling, 'individuals are able to learn positive out-group attitudes and intergroup behaviors from vicarious experiences portrayed by relevant others' and then apply them in different contexts (Vezzali *et al.* 2015, p.105).

And further results from the study showed 'that a structured intervention based on reading passages related to prejudice and conducted among Italian elementary school children improved attitudes toward immigrants (compared with a control condition where children read passages unrelated to prejudice) for children who identified more with the main positive character' (ibid.). The overall conclusions drawn and recommendations for practice were as follows:

> Educational interventions based on reading fantasy books that have characteristics similar to those of the Harry Potter series may improve relations with several types of stigmatized groups. The role of educators is particularly important for young children, for whom it might be more difficult to read individually and comprehend the meaning of complex books. In this case, educators can focus on specific passages strongly related to issues of prejudice... For adolescents and young adults, simply encouraging the reading of this type of book may be sufficient to improve out-group attitudes. Eventually, educators can organize discussion groups following the readings so as to reinforce their effects. (ibid.)

Results from previous research studies, some that date back 40 to 50 years, underpin the crucial need for diverse representation in literature. In a 1960s study carried out in the United States, 'white second graders who read stories from a multi-racial reader manifested more positive attitudes toward African Americans, including a greater tendency to identify with them and include them in their own group, than did those who read stories from a traditional reader where all the children were white' (Gray 2014). Another 1970s experiment, also conducted in the United States, showed that 'the attitudes of white children toward black children improved significantly as a result of hearing a story in which the protagonist was a black child' (ibid.).

Stories affect us all. Storytelling is not an exact science. We will not always be able to accurately predict what part of a story will appeal to the listener. We can never be certain as to what they will identify with in terms of experience or feeling, idea or thought. But what we can know is that by broadening their literary horizon, we increase the possibilities of this identification occurring. How staggering then are the opportunities we have, how huge a responsibility: to introduce children to multiple new worlds of ideas that have the power to change and to form them.

But how simple is it to source the diverse books we so evidently need?

In exploring this, I came across an article on a children's pop-up bookshop opened in Brixton, an area of London in the UK, in October 2018, featuring 'only books with black, Asian or minority ethnic (BAME) protagonists' (Flood 2018). The owners, Aimée Felone and David Stevens, reported how one customer visiting the shop burst into tears. Stevens, concerned as to her well-being, asked if she was alright and the customer responded by saying that she'd simply never before encountered anything like their store before. Having picked up six books in a row that all had brown faces on them, she had been moved to tears. Stevens' response in the moment was to apologize that it had taken such a long time for this to happen.

Felone and Stevens, independent publishers, opened their shop in response to a damning report from the Centre for Literacy in Primary Education (CLPE 2018), which found that 'of more than 9,000 children's books published in the UK in 2017, just 1% had a BAME main character' (Flood 2018). Felone reported children's excited responses to their offerings, saying, 'Mum this is me, this is me!' and remarked that it was moments like this that affirmed their reason for opening (Flood 2018).

'According to the CLPE report, just 4% – 391 – of the 9,115 books published in 2017 featured any BAME characters, compared with the 32.1% of schoolchildren of minority ethnic origins' (Flood 2018). The report states that, 'If in their formative years, children do not see their realities reflected in the world around them or only see problematic representations mirrored back at them, the impact can be tremendously damaging.' It tells publishers that 'to redress imbalances in representation is not an act of charity but an act of necessity that benefits and enriches all of our realities' (CLPE 2018, p.9). An updated CLPE report titled 'Reflecting Realities – Survey of Ethnic Representation within UK Children's Literature' published on the 11th of November 2020, says that the number of children's books featuring characters from a Black, Asian or minority ethnic background rose from 4% in 2017 to 10% in 2019 but that these characters remain significantly underrepresented when 33.5% of children in UK primary schools are from minority ethnic backgrounds (CLPE 2020). There was reportedly a small increase in the number of children's books published with an ethnic minority *main character*, a figure of 5% in comparison with 4% in 2018 and the 1% in 2017 previously mentioned.

The report also discussed findings where publishers revealed that '38% of their books featured animals or inanimate objects as main characters, meaning that children are almost eight times as likely to encounter an animal main character than a human main character who isn't white' (Flood 2020), which raises concerns in terms of reader identity and outlook.

A 2020 BookTrust report found that while there was some growth in the diversity of people working as authors and illustrators in the UK over the last two years, it was small. The figures indicated that in 2017, 6% of authors and illustrators from Black, Asian and ethnic minority groups created 4% of book titles, which rose to just under 9% creating 7% of titles in 2019 (Flood 2020).

Stevens, one of the store owners, mentioned the difficulty in finding books that are not only race specific but also more representative of issues such as class, gender and disability, commenting that they'd had 'to delve into backlists, the stock of tiny publishers and self-published books' (Flood 2018) in order to find them.

Not only is there a lack of availability in terms of books redressing the diversity imbalance, there is also bias in the existing literature. This bias runs not only along the lines of race, class and ability, but also gender. In a 2018 article in the United Kingdom's *Guardian* newspaper titled, 'Must Monsters Always Be Male? Huge Gender Bias Revealed in Children's Books', Donna Ferguson discusses an in-depth analysis of the hundred most popular children's books of 2017, carried out by the newspaper with the market research company Nielsen, which showed that:

- Twice as many of the characters given a speaking part and main role in a story were male.

- Male characters were often depicted in stereotypically masculine roles.

- Female characters were missing from a fifth of the books.

- Male villains were eight times more likely to appear than female ones.

- Male characters outnumbered female characters in almost half the stories that made it into the top hundred. Indeed, on average, there were three male characters present in each story for every two females.

- Only 40 per cent of characters in books were human. The rest were, 'for example, animals, birds, crayons, vegetables and skeletons. Among these creatures, the gender bias was even more marked. Whenever an author revealed a creature's sex, it was 73% more likely to be male than female' (Ferguson 2018).

- 'Males were more typically embodied as powerful, wild and potentially dangerous beasts such as dragons, bears and tigers, while females tended to anthropomorphise smaller and more vulnerable creatures such as birds, cats and insects' (ibid.).

- The depiction of female adults in caring roles was common in the stories, and 'there were twice as many female as male teachers. Mothers were also present almost twice as often as fathers. By contrast, fathers barely featured at all unless accompanied by a co-parent, appearing alone in just four books' (ibid.).

Jess Day, a campaigner with the Let Toys Be Toys movement, which aims to end gender stereotyping commented on the 'skewed' version of the world that this portrayal of gender represents, saying this 'is bad for boys as well as girls. The lack of fathers, for instance, steers them away from an interest in nurturing and caring behaviour' (ibid.).

In another startling find, a researcher and doctoral student by the name of Joseph McIntyre was motivated to analyse data on gender in children's literature when he realized that most of the characters in the books he was reading to his newborn daughter were male (Hough 2017). His findings on gender provided interesting insights into both representation in books and also in how books are used by different genders, showing that:

- Boys tend to 'check out books with male central characters much more than girls.

- About 77 percent of the books boys check out have only male central characters, 14 percent have female central characters, and 8 percent have both male and female.

- In contrast, the books girls check out are 51 percent female only, 42 percent male only, and 7 percent both' (Hough 2017).

McIntyre says that these findings show that 'there's evidence that on average girls are encountering a good number of characters of both genders while boys are almost only encountering books about boys. This preference for same-sex characters appears to grow as children age with boys in fifth grade almost only checking out books with male central characters' (Hough 2017).

Children's laureate Lauren Child, author and illustrator of the Charlie and Lola picture books, told Ferguson that the findings on gender communicate a message about how society views the female gender, 'If boys get the starring roles in books – both as the good and bad protagonists – and girls are the sidekicks, it confirms that's how the world is and how it should be. It's very hard to feel equal then' (Ferguson 2018). Nick Sharratt, another bestselling children's author and illustrator expressed surprise at the findings, explaining:

I do think about the ratio of male to female characters – I see it as part of the job. You never forget the picture books you enjoyed as a child. They stay with you for the rest of your life... Authors and illustrators have fantastic opportunities to break down stereotypes. We need to tackle these issues and at the moment it seems not enough is being done. (Ferguson 2018)

Not only is there work to be done in terms of book creation but also in terms of greater awareness of the existing bias and the finding of solutions, for example encouragement of more diverse book choices. As McIntyre says, 'I suspect that there are a lot of parents who want their boys to grow up respecting and appreciating girls and women… and exposing them to stories about girls and women could be a good way to start' (Hough 2017).

I would like to believe that it is most parents' wish for their children to grow up appreciating and respecting all people. And by drawing attention to the issue of diversity, we can actively work towards this goal. Change in this area will not be achieved by pretending that all people are the same. As Steele says, 'Children have some awareness of race from an early age, so research suggests that taking a colour-blind approach – or pretending that race doesn't exist – is not the best approach' (York University 2017). Indeed, if we consider how children learn, we will see that they are naturally immersed in the processes of discrimination and classification. They're constantly evaluating similarity and difference. Processes of differentiation are not problematic in themselves. Classification is problematic only when perceived differences are weighted with prejudical ideas. And these ideas are often communicated by adults who, at times, may represent certain groups of people as a standard with those who are different to this group as other. An interesting point to consider here is that otherness is relative; we are all 'other', depending on who we are engaging with. If I were to visit India, for example, I would be in the minority and the 'other'. If we can keep this in mind, it will aid us in celebrating all people, and presenting differences to the children in our care with respect and honour for all.

LEARNING FROM OTHER CULTURES

Another aspect of diversity in stories is the hidden messages they promote. A University of California team of researchers set up a study to explore how implicit lessons differed in storybooks from different countries (Cheung, Monroy and Delany 2017). They created a list of what they termed learning-related values, then checked to see how often the various books promoted them. Some of the values included:

- Goal setting to achieve something difficult.

- Putting in a lot of effort to complete a task.

- Generally viewing intelligence as a trait that can be acquired through hard work rather than a fixed quality from birth.

The findings, published in the *Journal of Cross-Cultural Psychology*, showed that the storybooks from China stressed the above-mentioned values at approximately double the frequency as the books from the United States and Mexico.

One example is a book deemed to be typical in China: *The Cat That Eats Letters*. The story is about a cat that has an appetite for sloppy letters – ones sized incorrectly, missing a stroke, etc. – with the only way for the children to protect their letters being to practise them daily and to write carefully. Psychologist Cecilia Cheung, a professor at the University of California, Riverside, explains that the underlying message, one of 'instilling the idea of effort – that children have to learn to consistently practice in order to achieve a certain level…is a core tenet of Chinese culture' (Aizenman 2018). Cheung and her collaborators analysed dozens of other storybooks from a list recommended by the education agencies of China, the United States and Mexico for the study, with this being just one example. Another example from China celebrates perseverance, not being distracted by others and staying on course to achieve your goals, with a contrasting example from the United States being a typical book called *The Jar of Happiness*. This is a story about a little girl who attempts to make a concoction of happiness in a jar, and when things do not unfold as she would like them to, she is upset until her friends step in to cheer her up. She ultimately realizes 'that happiness does not actually come from a jar of potion but from having good friends' (Cheung *et al.* 2017). Cheung explains that this emphasis on happiness is recurrent in many of the books from the United States, sometimes overt and sometimes subtle with 'drawings of children who are playing happily in all sorts of settings – emphasizing that smiling is important, that laughing is important, that being surrounded by people who are happy is important' (ibid). Interestingly, the same findings applied to the books from Mexico.

Cheung notes that children in China consistently achieve higher academic scores than children in both the United States and Mexico but says that this could be due to other cultural factors. Her takeaway from the study is the possibility that all three cultures should learn from each other. It is suggested that American parents may wish to 'supplement their children's reading with more tales that promote a view of intelligence as changeable' (Aizenman 2018), which helps children to persevere when faced with difficulty or failure. At the same time, Chinese parents could possibly learn from the American (and Mexican) focus on children's emotional states and the concern for their happiness (with it being an important factor in children's learning as well as a predictor of future success) as well as their prioritizing of a sense of connection to others.

The last two factors of diversity that we will explore are the access to the dominant literary culture of children's learning, and access to story where the literacy of parents and carers may be an issue. A 2015 paper on facilitating the smooth transition of children into formal schooling indicates that 'children familiar with the skills and knowledge associated with the dominant practices of literacy teaching in schools have an advantage' (Maher and Bellen 2015, p.9) with an easier passage into school (Hare 2011) is explored. The study notes that 'family attitudes to reading and writing have a defining influence on children's print knowledge and reading interest' (Weigel *et al.* 2010); and also there is often a disconnect between the home and community environments of minority children and those of formal schooling. With this in mind, literacy work before school entry is deemed to be crucial in terms of affecting outcomes.

The paper notes that the transition to school marks a change both in children's identity and status. They move from being 'a child to a pupil'. Along with this new identity, children also now need to navigate the ways in which learning is constructed and communicated. For many children from minority backgrounds their literary experiences are inconsistent with the literary practices they encounter on entry into formal schooling, which leads to a lack of success (Hare 2011; Hornberger 2009; Neuman 2006).

The paper considers the disappointing service of education systems around the world to Indigenous children, with their literacy achievement usually lagging behind that of their non-Indigenous peers. Some examples include:

- A 2009 Ministry of Education statistic in New Zealand that indicated a lower level of literacy for Maori children than for any other ethnic group at the end of their first year of schooling.

- A 2011 statistic in British Columbia, Canada, that indicated that in excess of 40 per cent of First Nations children did not pass the provincial reading test.

- In Australia, Aboriginal children, particularly those in rural areas, generally scored 'well below average in literacy benchmarks'.

(Maher and Bellen 2015)

These few examples form part of a 'growing body of research that emphasises the need for culturally appropriate programs for Indigenous children' (Maher and Bellen 2015, p.11), with members of these same communities highlighting the need for any such programmes to be both respectful and reciprocal in nature. The principles of culturally responsive teaching support this, specifying that 'the education of racially, ethnically, and culturally diverse students should connect in-school learning to out-of-school living; promote educational equity and excellence…and develop students' agency, efficacy, and empowerment' (Gay 2013, p.49).

The initiative we're discussing took place in six remote Aboriginal communities in the Northern Territory, Australia. The aim of the project was to 'empower…children to be able to staircase into formal schooling where literacy from a Western perspective would be dominant' (p.12). The research question that we'll focus on is the second question of the study which was, 'How can children's cultural capacity be built upon to enhance their literacy skills from a Western perspective?' (Maher and Bellen 2015, p.12). The study points out that the mere wording of this question honours the children's literacy capacity within their own culture and the learning that has already taken place.

The project began with contact between a non-Indigenous woman who was a university co-ordinator of the project and one of the authors of the paper, and the Elders in the community. Over time, the co-ordinator formed a connection with the Elders in order to discuss the project and to seek their input, leaving all final decision making with them.

The project sought to make 'Indigenous ways of knowing, being, and doing key pillars of children's learning' (Maher and Bellen 2015, p.13), building on positive aspects of their culture and negotiating with the community members regarding any innovation.

What the study found was that while the 'oral tradition in the community was extremely strong', and visual representation of ideas through artwork highly prized, there were few books available to the children. The lecturer, working with the preschool teacher (who had no formal qualifications but was a well-respected member of the community) discussed how they 'might bring the children's lived experience into the classroom' (Maher and Bellen 2015, p.14).

Together they decided that:

- All children would be given a disposable camera to take photos of things that interested them.

- The pictures would be uploaded into a computer and each child would dictate the text for an original book.

- Each child's book would be produced not only for them but also for all of their classmates.

- A 'big book' was made, containing all of the stories.

- A bookcase was provided to each household, and the children could take their own books and those of their friends home and keep them.

The findings showed that the children were enthusiastic about their books and were fascinated with the books of their friends too. They read the books to family members and, in turn, had them read to them. Many of the children had taken photos of the natural world that surrounded them; one had focused solely on body parts, some had taken photos of a fishing expedition and many had photographed the artwork of family members. A decision made by the Elders had been to ensure that the text was in both English and the children's own language in order to gradually improve their English ability prior to entry into formal schooling.

Further books were then made about a whole community expedition to the country: the traditional lands of the children and their families.

There, the 'Elders told Dreamtime stories…sang and danced' (p.14). The children were reportedly enchanted by the stories told. The photos taken were then used for the books, and the children were also enchanted by the books that were created. After these initial book projects it was possible to introduce commercially produced picture books into the preschool. 'Some of these, such as *The Naked Boy and the Crocodile: Stories by Children from Remote Indigenous Communities* (Griffiths 2011), about playing with friends, searching for emu eggs, hunting wild pigs and picking berries, were reflective of the local Indigenous culture' (Maher and Bellen 2015, p.14).

The initiative led to some impressive outcomes:

- The children had become extremely interested in reading, and in a preschool setting that implemented a free play philosophy, 'the children would choose to spend protracted periods reading, often in groups, talking and discussing, with deep concentration focussing on the fine detail of the pictures' (Maher and Bellen 2015, p.14).

- When a variety of children's picture books were provided as the final step in the process, the children were visibly excited about each new addition. Interestingly, 'these were English books and while no formal English competency pre- and post-assessment was undertaken with the children, anecdotally their English proficiency developed exponentially over the 2 years' (Steering Committee for the Review of Government Service Provision 2011, p.1723).

- Building on the children's cultural capital by respecting their 'ways of knowing, being and doing and making these a key pillar in the project' (Maher and Bellen 2015, p.14) was pivotal to the initiative's success. As described, the children were introduced to reading through a process of recording their daily lives, experiences and what was relevant to them in a traditional Western 'book', and then also recording different elements of their culture, such as dancing and the telling of their dreamtime stories. This use of their own culture and knowledge helped them to, over time, encounter the wonder of books and the sharing of knowledge with others through reading. In fact, the report states that 'in all the communities, making children's cultural knowledge a key pillar in their learning saw enhanced engagement with literacy activities' (Maher and Bellen 2015, p.15).

The initiative's findings and research indicate that effective literacy initiatives for Indigenous children should:

- be 'culturally safe' – that is, they should 'take into account cultural ways of knowing and working together with communities and families to build trusting partnerships that empower them to achieve commonly developed goals' (Maher and Bellen 2015, p.15)

- focus on children's specific cultural knowledge, as this is central to achieving positive literacy outcomes

- understand that having 'community Elders or family members as key contributors and affording them ownership of projects significantly contribute to the success of these programs' (p.16)

- include the involvement of staff, 'either Indigenous and who hold local knowledge, or non-Indigenous' who 'are trained in developing culturally relevant practice' (Maher and Bellen 2015, p.16)

- Make 'use of children's funds of cultural knowledge (Moll et al. 1992) from their home and community experiences to help validate their identity as competent and engaged learners' (ibid).

A transition into formal schooling can be successful for children from all cultural backgrounds, and it is story that can provide the cultural bridge. We all have stories to tell. Perhaps, as educators, we need to broaden our idea of what literary knowledge, literacy and reading are. I would propose that literacy is the communication of ideas first and foremost, and that if we can facilitate a joyful start on this journey by allowing the children to capitalize on their cultural knowledge – mainly through the sharing of their stories – in order to achieve success, then we will have set the stage for a lifetime of openness to the story process in all its forms, including formal literacy. And we will, as practitioners, be entering into a reciprocal learning partnership, one where we encounter new worlds as we truly listen to the children in our care.

The very last area we will be exploring in terms of diversity will be children's lack of access to literary content due to issues of illiteracy, and a possible solution that can be found in wordless picture books. In a 2017 dissertation paper for the University of Stellenbosch on how wordless picture books can be used to encourage parent–child reading in South Africa, the author Adrie le Roux described the state of the South African nation as follows: 14 per cent of the population were reported as reading often, and only 5 per cent of parents read to/with their children (Department of Basic Education 2015), and 51 per cent had no books in their home (South Africa Book Development Council 2007). A high percentage of South African children did not obtain basic literacy skills in their first three years at school (Department of Basic Education 2015) and there was a lack of parental involvement in providing cognitively stimulating activities to young children and engaging in these activities with them (Walker *et al.* 2007).

Many of the issues in South Africa can be attributed to the legacy of political issues that continue to affect the educational development of children long after the end of apartheid. Hull *et al.* (2003, p.6) discuss the work of Paulo Freire and the idea that language and literacy practices are inherently tied to 'identity issues, and identity issues…connect to issues of power, indexing one's position in relation to other individuals and groups socially and economically', with many learners having been 'oppressed, excluded or disadvantaged due to gender, ethnicity or social-economic status' (UNESCO 2006, p.152). Indeed, an inability to view 'books as a "cultural good"' (le Roux 2017, p.81) is explained by Professor M. Brown (Head of Department at the University of Pretoria's English Department) as 'one of the…legacies of Apartheid' (personal communication to le Roux, 5/9/2016).

Le Roux described the South African market as being dominated by English and Afrikaans picture books and, despite growing support for literary resources in the African languages, publishers are hesitant to publish such books for enjoyment due to the 'low buying power that the audience of these books may have' (le Roux 2017, p.6). The difficulties are further exacerbated 'by the large number of linguistic varieties and cultures in South Africa' (Johnson 2009, p.12) – 11 official languages in total – and the necessary awareness of different cultural conventions that is therefore essential in terms of meaning-making.

An interesting example of such a cultural convention is a local wordless picture book, *A Very Nice Day*, written by Ann Walton and Natalie Hinrichsen (2006). The book presents us with a visual narrative of a young African girl as she goes about her day: getting dressed, going shopping and returning home to make a meal. It is 'based in a typically South African milieu' (Ntuli 2011, p.257); however, it does not feature any parent or adult figure in a care-taking role:

> Readers who do not view these events as plausible may have a lower modality reading of the book, whereas children from a South African context, in which child-headed households are not uncommon, may be better able to relate to, believe and elaborate on the sequence of images. (2017, p.56)

And herein lies the difference between locally composed resources and those from abroad. Resources that allow for contemporary political, cultural and complex issues to be addressed are sorely needed. The beauty of the wordless picture book, in this instance, is that it can be used on both a simple level – shopping, cooking, basic hygiene, etc. – and a complex one, where the serious subject matter of child-headed households can be discussed.

Le Roux (2017, p.82) explains the importance of local context and meaning, stating 'The book cannot become a cultural good until its contents are relevant and suitable to the culture in which it needs to establish importance.'

Illiteracy can indeed prove to be 'an obstacle to fostering a love and culture of reading' (le Roux 2012, p.40) with parents and/or caregivers usually taking the role of children's primary educators, and then supporters in their literacy journey. However, le Roux (2017) explains that the active process of reading does not necessarily need to begin with written text as it includes visual perception and can actually be defined as 'an active, constructive, meaning-making process' (Colorado State University 2011). Radebe (in Morris 2007, p.33) 'believes that through the use of picture books, the illiterate parent is able to create a narrative via the contextual clues of the visual story. In this way, he or she is still able to share a rich experience with the child.' These wordless picture books, if produced in a culturally relevant and economically viable manner, could – 'through their ability to harness the tradition of storytelling' (le Roux 2017, p.11) and due to their unintimidating composition – begin to develop a reading culture. The resource provides hope for many parents who wish for their children to embark on a different educational journey to their own. A 2007 study (Seden 2008, p.137), indicated that many parents wanted to impart a love of reading for pleasure and education to their children and that this 'desire was irrespective of their own literacy background'.

The origin of wordless picture books extends back in time (Dowhower 1997, p.61). These stories formed from 'cave paintings to stained glass windows' (le Roux 2017, p.44). They are a natural form of communication: we simply need to consider how often children will draw illustrations in order to communicate stories when they are yet to develop the language to support their ideas. Wordless picture books function in much the same way as these rudimentary stories, lending themselves to the process of joint reading, which entails the exploration of images and the composition of stories. And this can all be done without any decoding knowledge or skill. Price, Van Kleeck and Huberty (2009, p.171) define book sharing as an activity 'during which parents mediate texts for young children, "scaffolding" their comprehension through interactions about the content and the illustrations and helping the child to participate in more sophisticated ways than he or she would be capable of independently'.

There is, on an international level, a large amount of literature which advocates for the use of wordless picture books in literacy development (Crawford and Hade 2000, p.67), and these resources have become a well-defined category of their own within children's literature and are considered to be beneficial in a number of ways. Some of these are:

- The fostering of connection between parents/caregiver and child due to their unique bond (Machado 2010, p.608):

  - A distinct advantage parents have is 'their ability to connect storybook features to personal experiences that they have shared with their child'. They also have the advantage of possessing 'insight into the distinctive character of their child – their traits, interests, desires and abilities' (le Roux 2017, p.78).

- The opportunity to 'expose children to "new worlds and concepts rarely used in everyday conversation or encountered in their everyday life"' (Louw and Louw 2014, p.177).

- The creation of 'a capacity for the child to interact with a range of literacies, to develop imagination and empathy' and it 'fosters the child's social, psychological and spiritual development' (Seden 2008, pp.134–135).

- The attunement of parents and caregivers to their children, which aids in early language development (O'Carroll and Hickman 2012, p.13) as does the necessity for the 'reader' to verbalize the narrative (Nikolajeva and Scott 2001, p.9). Perry Nodelman (1988, p.186) says that children tell 'the stories the pictures suggest to them; they themselves turn purely visual experiences into verbal ones'.

• The elevation of meaning-making is elevated due to the necessity to 'read' the images 'which consequently increases the need for the reader's involvement' (Arizpe, Colomer and Martínez-Roldán 2014, p.4). The reader, in fact, becomes central to the meaning-making process due to the lack of an author's voice.

• The fact motivation of 'reluctant readers' (Dowhower 1997, p.65).

• The accessibility provided to all readers regardless of their literacy level.

• The lack of 'right or wrong interpretation' which makes them less 'corrective by nature than books containing text', leading to more 'divergent types of thinking' (Crawford and Hade 2000, p.69).

• The worth they have 'when used with children from diverse circumstances' due to the fact that 'they enable the enjoyment of the same book by a variety of cultures' (Norton 1983, p.153).

• The opportunity they provide for readers to respond in their own ways which 'creates multiple narratives from the same book, as the genre does not prescribe a specific interpretation' (Williams 1994, p.38).

- The way in which they act as a 'subtle and complex art form that can communicate on many levels and leave a deep imprint on a child's consciousness' (Colomer, Kümmerling-Meibauer and Silva-Díaz 2010, p.1).

- The ability to simultaneously address different audiences through the sharing of, and appreciation by, children and adults at different levels of emergent reading (Jalongo *et al.* 2002, p.168) with each reader being able to construct their own interpretations.

- The necessity for the reader to be engaging in many actions concurrently, including 'identifying relevant signs, reconstructing sequences; creating or discarding hypothesis, and reading actively and collaboratively' (Bosch and Duran 2009, in Arizpe 2013, p.169, cited by le Roux 2017, p.62) and 'noting details, determining main ideas, making assumptions, drawing conclusions, noting cause and effect and making judgements' (Read and Smith in Whalen 1994, cited by le Roux 2017, p.63).

- The need for the reader to interpret the emotions of the characters in addition to their actions, leading to increased emotional awareness and literacy.

- The development of handling behaviours such as differentiating the front from the back of the book, learning to turn pages and navigate from left to right or right to left depending on the culture and language (Jalongo *et al.* 2002, p.168).

- The fact that many children are able to 'recognise, interpret and express themselves in pictures long before they master print' (ibid.).

- The development of 'inferential thinking and comprehension of story and visual discrimination' (Knudsen-Lindauer 1988, in Serafini 2014, p.25, cited by le Roux 2017, p.68).

- The fact that 'play with wordless books will often take the form of talking back to the book and entering the book...perhaps as one of the characters' (Sipe 2000, p.84).

- The opportunity they provide to contemplate and explore a text in terms of its 'potential meaning' which is a 'significant aspect of becoming visually literate' (Serafini 2014, p.26).

There is criticism of the genre with some arguing that, if misused, the books pose a threat to literacy. Nodelman (1988, p.1919) expresses concern that children may 'formulate a story whilst ignoring what the pictures essentially show' while Groff (1974, in Arizpe 2014, p.103) expresses concern about children being deprived of 'hearing literary language' which 'may hinder learning to read and literary appreciation'.

However, it would appear from the majority of le Roux's findings that wordless picture books are generally accepted as a beneficial medium in the development of literacy. The results of the study indicated that wordless picture books were indeed effective in that they encouraged 'a culture of reading in the home' and allowed for 'parents to contribute to their children's enjoyment of reading through the creation of stories using only pictures' as well as allowing for individual enjoyment (le Roux 2017, p.209). Due to their non-prescriptive nature, the books did prove to be a genre that could be used in a variety of languages, and by participants in different communities. In light of this, and the relative simplicity and affordability of the resource, it was felt by le Roux that these picture books can be regarded as particularly relevant in the South African context, considering the current reading crisis.

But it is not only South Africa where such a crisis exists. Many nations with diverse populations cater only for certain groups in terms of existing educational practices, with other peoples marginalized and excluded.

A group of empathetic individual stories will result in an empathetic collective story. (Helen Lumgair in Garnett 2017, p.166)

We tell children stories, not solely for the purpose of training them to be literate, but in order to build their understanding of the human experience. Through the give and take of listening and speaking, the accommodation of the ideas of others and the building and sharing of one's own, this construction occurs. Joan Almon, a Waldorf Early Childhood educator and co-founder of the Alliance for Childhood, in their article 'Oral Language: The Foundation of Literacy', for

Community Playthings (Almon n.d.), shares an anecdote that I found fascinating. She writes:

> Sometimes I heard children discussing a nursery rhyme, as we might discuss a piece of literature. On one memorable day, four-year-old Adam spoke to a friend about Humpty Dumpty. 'I don't think Humpty Dumpty fell,' said Adam. 'You don't?' replied his friend, in a tone implying a great heresy had been spoken. 'No, I think he jumped!'

How wonderful Adam's expression of his idea – yes, for him in terms of agency but more so for his friend – who may never have considered that Humpty had done anything but fall. This is the power of connection, of the collective; that by coming together, we are able to expand one another's thinking, leading to a greater abundance of ideas and possibilities.

And when we use story to uphold ideas of justice, cultivate compassion and foment hope in the individual lives of children, we foster these values in families, in communities, and in society at large. When we include the stories of all people, we make room for children to be altered by them: their thinking and feeling expanded. The autonomy and agency that story extend to us on an individual level can also function collectively: ideas and voices can be banded together to create shared stories, galvanize action and realize change as, for example, the Me Too movement has done (Me Too movement n.d.). As Paley (1990, p.34) says, 'An idea must find the rhythm of a group to be fully communicated. The imagination is not a unilateral function; it thrives in the company of those who share its point of view and ask the right questions.'

As individuals we form part of a collective: the dynamic, reciprocal flow of ideas and feelings in response to the stories of others and the expression of their own. Ensuring equality of access to stories, equality of agency in terms of expression of stories, and representation of all people will begin to change the story of the communities we live in, and in turn, society at large.

Chapter 8

Sensory Stories

JOANNA GRACE

WHAT IS A SENSORY STORY?

Sensory stories are a deceptively simple way of inclusively encouraging engagement with narrative. A sensory story is a *concise* text, usually between eight and ten sentences long, in which each sentence is partnered with a rich and relevant sensory experience appealing to a particular sensory system. They can be 'read' through the senses as well as through the text. You will have heard the old adage, 'A picture is worth a thousand words.' Well, consider how many words might be spoken by a smell, or even a taste! Through the course of a sensory story, you would expect to find sensations that appeal to seven sensory systems.

You may have heard of Storysacks or the company Bag Books. Both products involve sharing items with a child to enhance their engagement with story: small toys, pictures or tokens relating to a particular story are kept and revealed one by one as the story is told. If you've ever shared a Storysack with a group of children, you'll know what a powerful tool they are for encouraging engagement. A sensory story takes this to the next level. While a little laminated image of a character from the story (such that you might find in a Storysack) might appeal to a child, it is not much of a sensation, and so is relatively inaccessible to those story experiencers who have sensory differences. Offering the story through the senses makes it all the more interesting for typically developing children, while also making the story more accessible to those with physiological or neurological differences. For some children, making the story sensory is the difference between their being able to share the storytelling space with you, and their being completely excluded from that space.

WHAT CONSTITUTES A RICH AND RELEVANT SENSORY EXPERIENCE?

The richness of a sensory experience is something you need to judge through sensation alone. Consider a photograph: this is an interesting visual experience if you understand that the splodges of colour hold meaning. Your interest in it, although accessed through vision, is based in cognition. If you do not understand what the picture represents or if you are not curious about the image, then, viewed purely visually, it is simply a few small splodges of colour. Held up in a room it is far more likely that the light sources around, for example windows or illuminated bulbs, are visually more attractive. Sometimes, when seeking to judge what is an interesting visual experience, I will shake my head and attempt to blur my vision and notice what I can pick out from the milieu around me. It will be the bold neon colour of a particular toy, or the light from someone's phone screen. These are the things that draw the attention of our sense of vision.

As well as experiences that draw the attention of a sense, we can also look for sensations that fill an entire sense. An example of this for the sense of sight would be looking through a piece of coloured cellophane. Although this is an incredibly simple process, it changes everything you see. It is a massive visual experience.

If you are supporting people with profound disabilities or sensory processing difficulties, it can be worth exploring the development of each sensory system in detail, but to summarize briefly here: each one of our senses has a development process that it goes through.

SENSORY SKILLS – THE FOUNDATIONS OF LEARNING

Our later sensory skills are founded on our earlier sensory experiences. Exposure to a rich range of sensation in our early childhood is essential to the wiring of the brain, and children still mastering the use of their senses benefit from experiencing sensation at a level that is accessible to them. I often use mathematics as an analogy. I studied maths at university for a short while and took two A-levels in the subject. If I wanted to teach you maths I could write all the maths I know on a board and show it to you. Ta-da! This is maths. It is likely that if I did this, you would take a look at the board, jumbled with digits, equations, letters and complex formulae and decide, 'Maths is not for me!' You would disengage, and it is almost certain that you would be very unlikely to learn maths from this experience. For children still developing their mastery of a sense (for example their sense of sight), being exposed to the whole world of sensation, seeing the whole visual world, would place them in exactly the same position as you regarding that board of maths. They would be overwhelmed and would therefore disengage.

If I really wanted to teach you maths, I would likely start by giving you experience of 'one' and 'many'. We would move on to counting small numbers of objects and recognizing numerals. Then we would go on to addition, subtraction, multiplication, division and so on, continuing step by step until we were integrating, differentiating and manipulating complex formulae. You would be far more likely to learn to understand all the maths on the board if I was to take you through it in stages. It is the same for someone mastering sensation. Most typically developing children acquire the skills of using the information from their senses swiftly in the first few weeks of life but for some this process lasts longer, and for others it lasts a lifetime. The opportunity to access stimulation at an appropriate level allows for children to be included in life by meaningfully connecting, feeling and engaging, and understanding the development of the senses can therefore equip you to best support these children. For the purposes of telling a sensory story in a general setting, you need only to be thinking about providing rich sensations that draw the attention of a sensory system or fill a sensory system as we have seen above.

Of course, as well as being rich in sensations, the experiences you choose need also to be relevant to the part of the story they are about. The sensory experiences in a sensory story are not a side event: they convey the story as equal partners with the text. At first, this can seem strange. We often think of language as being of prime importance whereas language is just one of the tools we use to convey meaning. When you're thinking of developing literacy skills, it can be helpful to adopt an inclusive definition of literacy. If we define literacy as the sequencing and sharing of words, then we exclude from literacy those who cannot use words yet, or who speak another tongue, or who may never master traditional forms of communication.

However, if we define literacy as the sequencing and sharing of meaning, then we can include everyone in the storytelling space together. Consider the word 'run'. Just three little letters. How much of the meaning of 'run' is captured in three letters? Consider now the movement of running, itself a form of sensory stimulation. How much more does the movement of running mean 'run' than the letters? I'm not saying that sensation is always a better way of describing meaning than words, I am simply pointing out how powerful it can be. Poets use up a great many words trying to describe the beauty of a sunrise or the scent of a rose. How much more articulate is the visual experience of the sun rising, or the olfactory experience of smelling the rose?

I mentioned above that I would expect a sensory story to cover seven sensory systems over the course of its eight to ten sentences. You will have heard of the famous five senses, and you may be wondering how I arrived at seven. You may also be muttering that you have heard that there are nine sensory systems, or even eleven. You are right on all counts, as how we decide on our sensory systems is a little arbitrary, akin to deciding on how to group stars into constellations. If you wish to be technical, the human body has 33 sets of neurons that control its sensory systems, and so arguably we could say that we have 33 senses! I advocate for seven senses in a sensory story purely for pragmatic reasons as we need an achievable number within ten sentences. Eleven would be too many, nine would be ambitious and sensory systems such as our interoceptive system, which registers internal sensation, would be difficult or inappropriate for us to stimulate during the telling of a story. So the two additional senses I include in my sensory storytelling are the vestibular sense and proprioceptive senses.

SUBCONSCIOUS SENSORY SYSTEMS

Vestibulation

Your vestibular sense is your sense of motion and balance. Imagine yourself, for a moment, in a lift that has a silent motor and no windows. You know when the lift moves. You do not smell or taste the lift moving; you do not see the movement (as there are no windows); nor do you hear it (as this lift makes no sound). Your touch experience is simply your feet on the floor. However, you still know when the lift moves. It is your vestibular sense that informs you of the lift's movement. As with all of our senses, the ability to pick up sensory information and process it successfully is critical to our ability to access and engage with the world and with learning. The subconscious sensory systems are sometimes mistakenly viewed as less important than the conscious senses but this is not the case. If you lose your vestibular sense, this equates to paralysis. Without the ability to sense motion and balance, it is impossible to use motion and balance. The same is true for the next sense we will look at: proprioception. Again, without access to a functioning proprioceptive system you are unable to move.

Proprioception

Proprioception is your awareness of where your body is in space. Close your eyes, extend a finger and then, with eyes closed, bring your fingertip perfectly to meet the tip of your nose. Have a try. You may be successful or you may poke yourself in the cheek. How successful you are will depend on how well your brain is processing information from your proprioceptive sense. As you make this move, you are not feeling your way to your face, nor are you relying on touch or vision to partner your fingertip with the tip of your nose. What you are doing is using your awareness of where your finger is in space combined with your awareness of where your nose is. As proprioception and vestibulation are both critical for functional movement, moving is a great way to stimulate these senses. For proprioception, providing information about where the body is in space through other sensory experiences can heighten proprioceptive awareness. For example, if I had brushed your finger with a nail brush and brushed your nose with a nail brush prior to you completing my little task above, this would have heightened your awareness of where these body parts are.

Just as the value of the subconscious senses is not always appreciated in terms of their necessity to our basic functioning, the manner in which they underpin our access to education is also under-appreciated. It is clear how early visual experiences such as seeing the mark a crayon makes on a page motivate further exploration (that is, more mark-making), and this then becomes a skill like drawing, with writing skills developed at a later stage. With other sensations it is not as clear, and yet their foundational nature in terms of our ability to access our education is equally significant.

Childhood is changing in the modern world, and the range of sensations that older generations experienced when they were young is likely to be different to the range of sensations experienced by a child growing up today. If sensorial experiences have been missed, or have not been plentiful, then we would expect to see differences in the ability to tolerate and process sensations. These could appear as a disorder when, in fact, they are a deficit. For example, early vestibular development comes about through bold directional movement: we are rocked as tiny infants – from side to side or bounced up and down – and we are even thrown into the air and sometimes spun around and around. Did you ever roll down a sand bank or grassy hill or twirl yourself up on a swing and then unspin? A child who has not had access to this rich range of sensations, for example a child who has grown up with a lot of screen time, may not have spent much time rolling and spinning. It is not that the screen time has caused any damage, and some skills will certainly have been learned, but this screen activity will have displaced other activities that may have led to the development of important skills. You would expect a child with a deficit in early vestibular experiences to find it tricky to sit still, which is in itself an act of balance. If you can't sit still, your focus is taken up in trying to balance your body and you have less attention left over for visual focus. This may make it hard for you to focus on an object you are being shown. Although balance doesn't initially strike you as key to reading a book, it is actually an underpinning skill.

More children are being identified as having sensory difficulties, and therefore providing access to relevant sensation is rapidly becoming an essential part of early education. Giving this access to sensory experiences in a story format can help children who would otherwise be reluctant, or who would find it difficult to engage with the sensations, to become involved in the learning.

The sensory story below requires a little more preparation than the average story but would simply require gathering a few things from around your home and you would be ready to go. It is a beautiful story to tell, and if you are able to make the cardboard box books required to tell it, they can add to feelings of wonder and anticipation as you invite your children into the magical world of sensory storytelling.

A TROY TALE: SENSORY STORY

Introduction

A Troy Tale is based on real-life experiences. In 1971 librarian Marguerite Hart wrote to noteworthy individuals of the day inviting them to write letters to the children of Troy, Michigan, marking the occasion of the reopening of their library. The responses she received numbered close to one hundred, and included future presidents and famous actors, authors, artists and thinkers. The text of this story is based on what these noteworthy individuals wrote in their letters – especially Isaac Asimov – as they expressed their hopes for the children of Troy and their new library. They explained that the library was not just a library. It was, in fact, a time machine, a spaceship, a friend and a great many other marvellous things! Through sharing this sensory story you will be able to inclusively experience the pleasure of diving into a good book.

Resources

To share this story in a sensory way, you will need to gather the following items together before you begin:

Three boxes decorated to look like books – cereal packets or box files are ideal. Box folders work beautifully.

- Have fun decorating them with different textures and colours. See the suggestions below for how to decorate them to tie in with this story.

  - A ticking sound: you can use a wind-up clock or an egg timer, or simply a metronome app on a phone.

  - A sample of foods from around the world.

  - Something heavy that will fit inside a box, e.g. beanbags or bags of rice.

  - Paper scented with an invigorating fragrance/essential oil.

Optional

- Pictures of the people who wrote letters to the children of Troy or print-outs of the letters those people wrote.

Decorating the box books

Consider the richness of the sensations you can offer as you create these books.

Time Machine box book

Weight this box in any way that suits; for example you could secure a beanbag to the inside of the box or tape a wedge of paper inside. Decorate the outside of the box to give it a mechanical feel. Creating a collage of cogs, screws, nuts, bolts and circuit boards will give the box an interesting textured surface of cold hard edges for your story experiencers to feel.

Foods of the World box book

Decorate with the bright bold patterns of flags of the world. Hide the taste experiences you will be using to represent global travel inside this box.

Friend box book

Wrap the box in a fabric such as velvet or fleece to give it a soft, warm feel in contrast to the Time Machine box.

How to share the sensory story

- Prepare all your resources and lay them out somewhere you will be able to reach them easily as you tell the story.

- To tell the story, read each section in turn, taking time to share the words slowly and expressively, allowing the children to ask questions or add their own insights.

- After you have shared the words of a section, offer the partnered sensory experience for the children to feel. Allow time for the feeling and processing of the experience. Remember this is about sensation and not language so do try to hold back from using too much language at this point. Join in with feeling the sensation – modelling how to engage with sensation – just as you would model how to engage with text.

- The story is told from the point of view of one of the children of Troy who has grown up to be an author, and is remembering their experiences in the library when they were a child. The conciseness of the text leaves lots of opportunities for children to enrich the story with their own insights, to ask questions and be curious.

A Troy Tale

Isaac, Neil, Theodor and nearly one hundred other great men and women wrote to me when I was a child.

16 March 1971

Dear Boys and Girls,

Congratulations on the new library, because it isn't just a library. It is a space ship that will take you to the farthest reaches of the Universe, a time machine that will take you to the far past and the far future, a teacher that knows more than any human being, a friend that will amuse you and console you ---and most of all, a gateway, to a better and happier and more useful life.

Isaac Asimov

Sensory experience

- Around the room pin pictures of the people who wrote letters to the children of Troy or print-outs of the letters those people wrote (or hold them up).

- Spin your story experiencers slowly as if showing them a crowd of people all around them. As the child turns they will see all of the people.

- Encourage story experiencers who enjoy spinning a lot to spin first one way and then the other. This offers your story experiencers stimulation to their vestibular sense.

They all told me to go to the library and read, read, read!

Sensory experience

As you say 'read, read, read' bring out the box books and stack them in front of your story experiencers as if setting them the task of reading each one.

The rhythm of your words combined with the beat of the books being stacked one by one provides your story experiencers with stimulation to their auditory sense. With this sensation you provide the stimulation simultaneously with the words of the text.

So I went…

Sensory experience

Present your story experiencers with the first of your box books, the Time Machine box book: the heaviness of the box will stimulate their proprioceptive sensory system and can signify the weight of knowledge to be found within a library.

Inside I discovered a time machine
Sensory experience
Support your story experiencers in opening the Time Machine box book, in doing so they will experience the tactile qualities of the box.

It is the same time machine that I am using to travel back and meet with you today

Sensory experience
Hear a ticking sound representing time passing.

I opened a book, but it wasn't a book, it was a teacher
Sensory experience
Present your story experiencers with the second box book – the Foods of the World box book. Allow them time to explore the exterior of the box through touch and sight.

And it taught me about the world
Sensory experience
Invite your story experiencers to open the box and sample the foods from around the world that you have placed inside. Another way to do this is to tell the story on several occasions, and on each retelling share

a different food. In this way your story experiencers have the opportunity to enjoy a wide range of experiences but you do not have to try and balance a multitude of different taste experiences carefully within the box.

An alternative to providing food (if it proves too difficult) is to provide the smells of different foods. You can provide the smell of food by presenting flavourings, or using herbs and spice, or simply using a small amount of a particular food. (You will find that warming up a scent helps it to become more potent.)

I took another book from the shelf and brought it home with me

Sensory experience

Present the final box book to your story experiencers for them to explore through their sense of touch.

Where it became a friend

Sensory experience

Have your story experiencers hug the soft, cosy book, or invite your story experiencers to wrap their arms around themselves and embrace themselves in a big hug or to hug each other if they are able to. A hug is a wonderful sensory experience for reinforcing proprioceptive awareness.

Finally I poured my mind and spirit into books and stored them up here in the library for you
Sensory experience
Lay out the fragranced paper before your story experiencers in a place where they will be able to smell it, act out the furious scribblings of an impassioned writer and place the written-on pages into or onto the box book pile.

The narrator of A Troy Tale was one of the children who received the letters when the library of Troy reopened. They were so inspired by their early visits to the library that they went on to become a writer themselves. You can end this story by encouraging your story experiencers to follow suit and inviting them to begin to compose their own stories to add to your library. They can mark-make or write on the fragranced paper. (Writing on smelly paper is often a lot more motivating than writing on ordinary paper!)

Extension/Further activities

- Mark-make or write on scented paper and contribute your pages to a class book.

- Write letters to future generations explaining what is to be found in a library or ask people you know and respect to write such letters to you.

- Find out about everyone's favourite food and bring in tastes to share. Has anyone travelled to a different country? What kinds of foods did they eat there?

- Create a library of sensory box books, to be read with all the senses. Create books on different topics; for example, a book about swimming might contain a swimming hat, some anti-chlorine shampoo and be decorated with the sort of mosaic tiles that line a pool. A book about a farm might contain the smell of animal feed, the feel of different animal hides, the sounds of mud squelching and hooves clip-clopping. Invite children to create sensory books about people they know or activities they enjoy. Write a sensory story about a class trip. Work together to identify the sounds, smells, sights, etc. that you experience on your trip and collect these in your box book.

- Use a washing line to 'write' a sensory story by clipping items of differing sensory interest onto it. 'Read' the line by experiencing the sensations in sequence from left to right. You can use a washing line like this to do sensory cloze exercises, as you would with written cloze exercises where a sentence is presented with a word missing and a selection of possible words to fill the gap. Remove a sensory item from your sensory washing-line sentence and present it with a couple of other objects. Then invite children to choose the appropriate item to complete the sensory sentence.

- Ask the children whether they have ever travelled through time in a book. Create a timeline of books that you have in class to show the children how far they can travel. For example, you might place a book about dinosaurs at the start of the timeline and one set in the future at the other end.

- Explore with the children what they could learn through reading books. It could range from how to bake a cake to speaking a different language or doing a particular craft.

FINDING OUT MORE ABOUT SENSORY STORIES

If you would like to find out more about sensory stories and sensory storytelling, my book *Sensory Stories for Children and Teens with Special Educational Needs* (Grace 2014) goes into detail about the value of the approach and contains five sensory stories with associated activities. The Sensory Projects publish a range of sensory stories. If you visit www.thesensoryprojects.co.uk, you can download a free basic guide to sharing sensory stories that provides information on how to get the most out of your sensory story sharing, including additional information for people planning on sharing sensory stories with individuals with additional needs, for example children with autism or profound disabilities. The CPD-accredited course 'Ambitious and Inclusive Sensory Storytelling' teaches delegates how to maximize the impact of their sensory storytelling and reveals the power of sensory stories as a tool for inclusion. But, for now, what better way to find out how to use one than to go ahead and try one?

Chapter 9

The Stages of Story – A Model

A story beckons us to lose ourselves in wonder as we begin to absorb it and to consider it in multiple ways through a wide range of cognitive and emotional responses.

In a paper by the Center for Universal Education at the Brookings Institution titled 'Learning to Leapfrog: Innovative Pedagogies to Transform Education', the authors discuss the current global learning crisis: that is, that a great deal of teaching 'is not succeeding in embedding the knowledge, skills, and dispositions that societies and economies demand' (Istance and Paniagua 2019, p.8). The authors state that 'many educators argue that the best way for schools to prepare young people for future success is to help them develop a broad range of learning, work, and life skills that they can deploy all their lives, regardless of what the future entails' (p.9). However, what is needed is not only breadth of knowledge and skills but also depth: the deep understanding necessary in order to solve problems and to transfer knowledge, which means 'using teaching and learning approaches that enable students to delve deeply into subjects' (p.9).

The paper considers some playful and engaging approaches to learning which allow for this deep engagement, with the four that are the most interest in terms of story being:

- experiential learning
- embodied learning
- multiliteracies
- gamification.

Experiential learning describes approaches that understand learning as a social activity, with human experience at the centre and learners in direct contact with what is being studied, for example project-based or inquiry-based learning. Cathy Hirsh-Pasek, a professor of psychology at Temple University and co-author of *Becoming Brilliant: What Science Tells Us About Raising Successful Children* with Roberta Michnick Golinkoff, reports that one of her friends refers to the human brain as a 'socially gated brain' (Turner and Kamenetz 2019). Hirsh-Pasek, who has been studying childhood development for almost 40 years, explains why the friend uses this term, saying that, 'Everything goes through the social. Everything we learn starts with collaboration and relationships (Turner and Kamenetz 2019). Due to the informal and social nature of experiential learning, children's own experience, skills and tacit knowledge can be included in the process and this helps to foster 'a sense of identity and belonging' (Istance and Paniagua 2019, p.23) as they learn.

Embodied learning 'builds on research showing the involvement of the physical body and activity in learning' (p.25). Istance and Paniagua explain: 'when cognition is underpinned by the act of creating something to foster self-expression, learning can become a creative experience and engage students' (p.25). As the late Bev Bos (quoted by Lumgair in Garnett 2017, p.159) said when discussing movement and learning, 'If it hasn't been in the hand…and the body…it can't be in the brain!'

Multiliteracies as a pedagogy challenge the conception of literacy as only basic reading and writing skills (which we've briefly considered), including different modalities in order to provide learners with ways in which to express their multilingual and multicultural identities. The New London Group explain that:

> Multiliteracies are related to multimodality, as many modes are encouraged to be used in different forms of expression… This differs widely from traditional classroom pedagogy that is often focused on monomodal tools for learning and which does not include a range of perspectives, which can result in a lack of cultural and linguistic diversity represented in teaching approaches. (David 2020)

It has been shown that multiliteracies 'increase learner's cognitive engagement and agency in literacy practices', allowing them to act as 'competent contributors' (Istance and Paniagua 2019, p.29). Language is also an important part of the multiliteracy approach with mother-tongue and bi/multilingual education being repeatedly identified as 'among the most effective practices in developing countries and in the education of diverse communities' (p.28), often revitalizing Indigenous languages and counteracting 'deficit approaches' (p.29) to languages used by minority groups.

Gamification looks to blend ability, motivation and enjoyment in order to encourage students to fully engage in an activity. It is not only about games and their design, but about capturing 'the underlying benefits of game mechanics to immerse students in learning' (Istance and Paniagua 2019, p.31). *And one of the key components of gamification is storytelling.* Storytelling is crucial in terms of situating learning, helping children to 'create a mental model of an entire process' and to 'maintain their attention as they want to know what happens next' (p.31). Research has shown that not only does gamification enhance 'engagement and motivation, social relations and satisfaction' (p.32); it also:

- aids in comprehension

- reinforces positive attitudes towards learning

- helps retention and recall

- encourages critical thinking

- develops social and cognitive skills

- builds community among students and teachers

- enhances memory recall

- supports early literacy development

- promotes creative thinking.

The story process encompasses each one of these pedagogical approaches which aid children's learning by actively involving them in their learning, and empowering and emboldening them in terms of their existing and developing skills.

THE STORY PROCESS

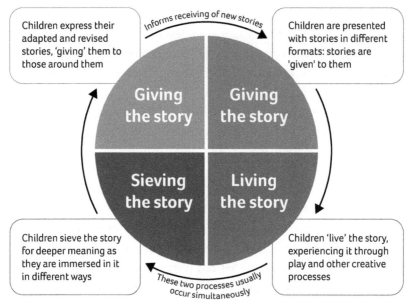

Figure 9.1 The narrative process

Giving the story

The process of story is a cyclical one. For the purpose of our learning we'll consider the sharing of story with children as the initial story stage. This is when the children receive information presented in a narrative form. As a story unfolds, children mostly focus their attention and listening, beginning to absorb the story ideas. Agosto (2016) discusses storytelling as, at times, being 'so powerful that students can enter a trance-like state when deeply listening'.

We therefore need to consider the manner in which we deliver a story. Do we tell and read with passion and excitement? Do we convey a sense of curiosity? Do we exclaim and marvel? Do we celebrate surprise and discovery? More importantly, do we honour the contributions of the children?

As we allow children time and space to listen and to absorb the story content without pressure, and as we model honouring the contributions of others, we provide them with a sense of security that will encourage them to slowly volunteer ideas of their own. For those who are eager to contribute, we can gently invite them to elaborate on their feelings and thoughts.

As we share ideas, it is essential for us to remember that no idea or suggestion is 'wrong'. If a child expresses something inappropriate, we can gently acknowledge what they've said or even that they've made a contribution, and wisely steer the conversation along, returning to address their comment on an individual basis where necessary (following child protection guidelines if the matter is deemed as serious). As we acknowledge their contributions, children will feel that they are competent partners in the story process, leading to increased participation.

Meghan Cox Gurdon (2019) speaks about children benefiting when 'they and their parent establish a positive pattern of relating while reading' (Dickinson *et al.* 2012, p.3) which leads to the regulation of attention. Vivian Gussin Paley, in *The Boy Who Would Be A Helicopter*, refers to her own attempts to stop interruptions during storytelling before coming to understand it as a shared process. She explains:

> In storytelling, as in play, the social interactions we call interruptions usually improve the narrative. Yet I can recall a time when I would say, 'Please don't interrupt. Let people tell their own stories.' That was when I missed the main point of storytelling. I did not understand it to be a shared process…the social art of language. (Paley 1991, p.23)

In an article in the United Kingdom's *Guardian* newspaper on the killing of curiosity in schools, Wendy Berliner describes curiosity as one of the 'critical methods humans adopt to learn' and explains that the promotion of 'curiosity is a foundation for early learning that we should be emphasising more when we look at academic achievement' (Berliner 2020). She considers research carried out in 2007 that entailed researchers logging the questions asked by children between the ages of 14 months and 5 years, which amounted to an average of 107 per hour (Chouinard, Harris and Maratsos 2007), and contrasts this with research from Susan Engel (2011), a leading authority on curiosity in children who found that 'questioning drops like a stone once children start school' (Berliner 2020). In her findings, when 'her team logged classroom questions, she found the youngest children in an American suburban elementary school asked between two and five questions in a two-hour period. Even worse, as they got older the children gave up asking altogether. There were two-hour stretches in fifth grade (year 6) where 10- and 11-year-olds failed to ask their teacher a single question' (ibid).

These findings should cause us to feel some sense of alarm. Loris Malaguzzi, founder of the Reggio Emilia approach, said in an interview:

> The child dies if we take away from him the joy of questioning, examining, and exploring. He dies if he does not sense that the adult is close enough to see how much strength, how much energy, how much intelligence, invention, capacity and creativity he possesses. (Rinaldi 2006, p.42)

The collaboration that the story process lends itself to matters to children. Paley explains it thus:

> Friendship and fantasy form the natural path that leads children into a new world of other voices, other views and other ways of expressing ideas and feelings they recognize as similar to their own... To children, each new revelation of connectedness is a miracle. (1991, p.34)

Not every one of us feels comfortable telling stories. For some people it appears effortless and easy, a natural process. For others, it is something that requires effort and practice. In a 2014 article 'Why Storytelling in the Classroom Matters', Matthew James Friday writes about how teachers are storytellers, and storytellers teachers. He discusses the effectiveness of interactive storytelling, reporting that he doesn't rely on merely speaking the story while sitting still, but rather is physically active: using pace, moving around and gesturing. He also invites children from the audience to be involved in the story, by asking them to act out parts of the storyline, repeat dialogue and use props. And he also stops and starts 'the story a lot, asking the audience to contribute sound effects, to answer questions, to make suggestions' (Friday 2014).

Some of his ideas for becoming a better storyteller include:

- Reading as wide a variety of story materials from across the globe as you can: fables, folktales, myths, legends, etc.

- Watching professional storytellers and learning from their different styles.

- Building confidence through the use of different voices as you engage in picture and chapter books.

- Stopping to ask questions as you tell or read stories; creating a shared event by making the story as interactive as possible.

- Writing stories down in a notebook (which aids in recall) and modelling this for the children.

- Not expecting perfection when telling stories – having scripts or books nearby to help and to prompt you.

- Building a prop box by collecting bits and pieces that can help to bring the story process to life.

(Friday 2014)

Stories are precious. We need to ask ourselves if we carry the weight of the wonder of story with the gravitas it deserves, demonstrating a love for the possibility it holds to transform us all. We are privileged to bear the gifts of story each day, presenting children with what may be known to us but is often a complete mystery to them…a road not yet travelled. And it is they who enrich the story process. They can teach us, as adults, more about the stories we tell them. Let's be humble in our approach, eagerly awaiting the children's responses, allowing them at times to guide us with their responses. Let's dance down this avenue of discovery together joyfully.

Living the story

When choosing stories and presenting them to the children, we can begin to think about how to explore them further. Helen Garnett, author of the book *Developing Empathy in the Early Years: A Guide for Practitioners*, coined the term 'living the story' for a process where children 'reflect on the story during circle time, small group discussions or through one-to-one interaction with the teacher'. Through this exploration they 'are able to discuss, debate, anticipate, and hypothesize about alternative endings. They create artwork based on the story; they play with objects from the story, and they role-play using characters from the story. They act, sing and dance' (Garnett 2017, p.159). What is needed to do this on a practical level is time, space and resources. There is no need for resourcing to be elaborate or expensive. We can use existing toys, books and supplies for arts and crafts, as well as recycled materials. The children will not be looking at what the items are but rather considering how they can be used in their processes of story and play. In many instances the simpler the resource the better the ideas generated.

In an example of this, Wendy Berliner writes about Susan Engel's September 2019 visit to Ilminster Avenue nursery school in Bristol, where the nursery had taken 'the radical step of permanently removing most of its toys for two-year-olds and replacing them with a range of cardboard boxes, tin cans, pots and pans, old phones, kettles, computers and plumbing supplies – anything with creative possibilities' (Berliner 2020).

> The children took to the new objects immediately, making slides for building blocks with guttering, dens and spaceships with cardboard boxes and having conversations with imaginary people on old phones. Old keys were used to lock things away or unlock imaginary kingdoms. (Berliner 2020)

The headteacher reported that most children had not asked for the old toys back, and though initially sceptical, the parents and teachers had 'been convinced by the change because of the rise in creativity and conversation among the children' (Berliner 2020).

The process of 'living the story' is one where children have the freedom to create. We tend to think of creativity as something that only certain people possess, a disposition that they are born with. However, creativity can be fostered and developed in the lives of all children, both through their interactions with others and through their environment. Andreas Schleicher, Director for the Directorate of Education and Skills at the Organisation for Economic Cooperation and Development says that PISA (the OECD'S Programme for International Student Assessment), conceptualizes creative thinking as 'the competence to engage productively in…the generation, evaluation and improvement of ideas that can result in novel and effective solutions, advances in knowledge and impactful expressions of imagination' (Schleicher 2019, p.12). In terms of young children's learning, these processes can all be found in play. The repetition, the evaluation of existing ideas with frequent improvements and adaptations, and the generation of completely new ideas are both underpinned by imagination and further aid in its development, as well as aiding in the advancement of knowledge. Dr Helen Charman, Director of Learning and National Programmes at the Victoria and Albert Museum, says that 'play is how we try ideas on for size, how we test and experiment with "what might be"; how we make connections between ideas, people and things', and goes on to describe how

> this ability to act in and on the world – let's call it *creative agency* – is vital for every young person's education today, because the world which they inhabit and will inherit is faster-moving, and more complex and uncertain, than perhaps at any time before. (Charman 2019, emphasis mine)

Michael Rosen discusses creativity, saying, 'Whenever I work with people – no matter what their age – I try to run a checklist through my mind: are these people investigating, discovering, inventing and cooperating?... In my experience, things start to happen when all four take place in a group of people' (2010, p.14). Let's explore this in further detail.

INVESTIGATION

For children, play and story are melded together in fantasy, and they use this dual system to investigate their world and to navigate the knowledge they acquire. Peter Gray says:

> I would put it this way. Stories are a form of play, and, as in all play, our involvement with stories is a way of acquiring skills and ideas that are valuable for negotiating the real world. When we enter into a story we enter a make-believe world where, precisely because it is make-believe and has no immediate real-world consequences, and because the events are simplified and the important ones made salient, we can experience the challenges and difficulties more clearly, think about them more rationally, and develop more insight about them, than we might from real-world experience. (Gray 2014)

Lovegreen and Lumgair (2016, in Garnett 2017) describe the merging of story and play thus:

It is through play that we take what we know, what we hear, what we and those close to us experience, and add it to our story. There is thinking involved. We see the cause and effect of our decisions. There is feeling involved. We feel the emotional responses of our decisions... both thinking and emotions are the main characters in the powerful processes of story and play. (p.160)

The cognitive processes underpinning play are many. As children engage in dramatic or make-believe play scenarios, the following processes are at work:

- Working memory – to remember the roles of the children who are participating as well as the continuing story narrative (Thompson 2009).

- Inhibition – to remain in role rather than enacting another child's role or becoming distracted by other classroom activities (ibid.).

- Cognitive flexibility (to adapt to changes in the evolving plot and to provide 'stage directions' to other children while maintaining one's own role in the play) (ibid.).

- Increased 'language usage' (Kaufman 2012).

- The important concept of Theory of Mind, 'an awareness that one's thoughts may differ from those of other person's and that there are a variety of perspectives of which each of us is capable' (Kaufman 2012, citing Jenkins and Astington 2000; Leslie 1987; Singer and Singer 1990).

- 'Cognitive integration of seemingly separate content' (Russ 2004, n.p.).

- 'Divergent thinking (the ability to come up with many different ideas, story themes, and symbols)' (ibid.).

- 'Enhancement of the child's capacity for cognitive flexibility and ultimately, creativity' (Kaufman 2012, citing Russ 2004; Singer and Singer 2005).

The following affective processes happen simultaneously:

- 'Expression of both positive and negative feelings' (Kaufman 2012).

- 'Modulation of affect' (ibid.) – this is the ability to adapt and vary the strength of one's emotional state in order to meet the demands of an environment (children who are able to do this will be able to flexibly adapt to a range of emotionally stressful situations).

- The integration of 'emotion with cognition' (ibid., citing Jent, Niec and Baker 2011; Seja and Russ 1999; Slade and Wolf 1999).

- The development of 'self-regulation including reduced aggression, delay of gratification, civility, and empathy' (Kaufman 2012).

How do we further facilitate the investigation of story with children effectively?

- We allow them to step outside of themselves and imagine what it's like to be a different character. Michelle Borba in *UnSelfie* writes about a high school English teacher in Oregon, United States, who helps her ninth-grade students to understand the perspective of different characters by using paper shoe cutouts. 'Her test for Shakespeare's *Romeo and Juliet* is for students to take turns stepping onto each cutout and describing that character's views and feeling.' The teacher says that 'the exercise not only enhances her students' perspective for each character, but…also is their favourite test' (Borba 2016, p.82). Borba also talks about a mother in Liverpool who carries out a similar, powerful exercise but using real shoes. Borba explains, 'When her family finished reading *Charlotte's Web*, she printed each character's name…on a sticky note and stuck them on her husband's shoes. Her kids were delighted to jump into each big shoe and pretend to be the character' (p.83).

- We allow for story discussion with both peers and practitioners, and extend this by encouraging story discussion with parents and carers.

- We help in creating rhymes, poems and songs and encourage expression in a broad variety of modalities.

- We listen carefully to the stories created, acting as scribe when the children wish to communicate the stories in print.

- We facilitate hypothesis('what if?') questions and scenarios, running through the children's imaginings with them, aiding them in *their* adaptation and restructure of stories.

- We allow for fun and incorporate humour as children play. Humour may not be something that comes to mind when we think about learning but it has been shown to be a motivating factor in the learning process (Bellace 2011) and 'a critical skill in thought, communication and social interaction' (Garnett 2017, p.163). Young children are drawn to humour because 'humor, as a form of play, provides children opportunities for playful manipulation of the real world' (Garnett 2017, p.163, citing Kolb 1990).

- We gently join in when asked to do so (and only in the capacity children wish for us to fill, under their guidance and direction).

Kaufman reports that 'A school atmosphere in which pretend games are encouraged, or even just tolerated in the curriculum or recess play of children, has…been shown to lead to even greater amounts of imaginativeness and enhanced curiosity' (Kaufman 2012, citing Ashiabi 2007; Singer and Lythcott 2004). Anna Craft, in her paper 'Creativity and Possibility in the Early Years', says that,

> as children contribute to the uncovering of knowledge, they take ownership of it. When control over the investigation of knowledge is handed back to the child, they have the opportunity and authority to be innovative. A learner-inclusive approach, then, includes children in determining what is to be investigated, and values their experiences, their imagination and their evaluation. (n.d., p.4, citing Jeffrey 2001; Jeffrey and Craft 2004)

Children love to investigate their world. They are curious, imaginative and creative. We can amplify these qualities simply by affording them the room to take charge.

DISCOVERY AND INVENTION

I've chosen to discuss these two processes together due to the fact that they are intertwined in children's play. Thomas Hobson, known as 'Teacher Tom', says that:

> Children should be able to do their own experimenting...their own research. Teachers...can guide them by providing appropriate materials, but the essential thing is that in order for a child to understand something, he must construct it himself, he must re-invent it. (Hobson 2019)

As we provide children with the riches of story and the room for role-play, they become fully absorbed in worlds of their own creation. And this 'process of creativity' where children go 'further than the information given, to create something new and original for them', can be deemed as important to them 'as any product they may create' (Duffy 2010, p.20).

Professor Mihalyi Csikszentmihalyi, who spent many years studying states of optimal experience in adults (times when the adults reported feelings of intense concentration and deep enjoyment), 'has showed that what makes experience genuinely satisfying is the state of highly creative consciousness, which he also calls "flow"'. He says that 'perhaps the state that we most associate with childhood "flow" is that of play', which seems to invite 'children to interact in unique ways with the environment', explaining that the activities that are most effective 'seem to need to be originated by the individual and to be open-ended, with the outcome determined by the participants' (Ellyatt 2010, p.91). Ellyatt explains this as children striving to be 'the causal agents in their own environments: creating their own answers, to enjoy problem-solving for its own sake' (p.92).

McNamee (2005) describes how Vivian Gussin Paley's study of children's play brought her closer to their point of view, 'their questions and working hypotheses regarding human nature, good and evil, the ups-and-downs of relationships, and how materials and people work' (p.278). It is through these exercises in imagination that children are discovering the world, both the outer world consisting of their immediate culture and community and beyond, and their inner world. Hearn (1992, cited in McNamee 2005, p.285) describes stories as 'patterns that identify shapes of human behavior, patterns that lead to understanding a random world, and ultimately, patterns that lead to understanding [ourselves]. They make culture make sense.'

But even more important than what it is that children are discovering, and inventing, is that through this marriage of story and play they *are* discovering and inventing. McNamee (2005, p.288) cites Paley (2005, p.26), who believes that the focus of fantasy play 'rather than being a distraction, helps children achieve the goal of having an open mind', further stating that 'developing relationships and ideas in play opens the mind to possibilities'.

In a paper titled 'Pedagogy and Possibility in the Early Years', possibility thinking is defined as 'imagining what might be' (Cremin, Burnard and Craft 2006, p.2). The authors believe that possibility thinking is 'exemplified through the posing, in multiple ways, of the question "what if?"' and that it involves the shift from 'what is this and what does it do?' to 'what can I do with this?' (Cremin *et al.* 2006, p.2, citing Jeffrey and Craft 2004), the core areas of possibility thinking in the context of children's learning identified as:

- the posing of questions

- play

- immersion and making connections

- the use of imagination

- intentionality

- innovation

- risk taking

- self-determination.

(Cremin et al. 2006, p.3)

Craft says that 'possibilities are generated by children (and adults) in all areas of learning, whether imaginative play, musical exploration and composition, cooking, mark-making or writing, outdoor physical play, mathematical development or early scientific enquiry' (Craft n.d., p.1, citing Craft 2000, 2001, 2002). We witness these processes as the children take a story and begin to live it. Their use of imagination seems effortless as they immerse themselves in the fantasy process, connecting all that is familiar and unfamiliar to them in innovative ways. They take risks as they continually ask 'what if' in their play, reinventing and creating alternative characters, plots, actions and endings. They are the drivers of their learning, intentional in the execution of their ideas.

Craft (n.d.) says that this 'possibility thinking is at the heart of all creativity in young children, whether they are working alone, in parallel or in collaboration with others' (p.1). And this dramatic play often begins with phrases such as 'Let's pretend...', which McNamee describes as 'the entry point to abstract logical thinking' (McNamee 2005, p.282).

CO-OPERATION

Co-operative partnerships are essential to the development of young children. The relationships between children and their parents, their practitioners, their peers and 'people who are significant to the child' (Smith *et al.* 2003, p.495) provide the context for this development. '[Vygotsky's] theory stresses the role of interpersonal processes and the role of society in providing a framework within which the child's construction of meaning develops' (p.495), with the idea 'that the human mind itself "extends beyond the skin"' (Wertsch and Tulviste 1996, p.60, cited by Smith *et al.* 2003, p.499). Rogoff and her colleagues (1995) further developed 'the Vygotskian idea that individual cognitive development is inseparable from interpersonal and community processes' (Smith *et al.* 2003, p.505). Piagetian researchers like Willem Doise and Gabriel Mugny showed that:

> Children working in pairs or small groups come to solve problems more effectively than when they work alone. The reason seems to be that it is through social interaction that they come to see the solution. When the child encounters conflicting views this stimulates internal disequilibrium that the child is motivated to resolve. (Smith *et al.* 2003, p.514)

Let's consider this co-operation in light of the story process. McNamee, discussing Paley's work, says that 'Storytelling, story acting, and listening to stories provide the most successful discourse format for young children; stories generate dialogue where young children are eager for all the talking and listening they can receive and give' (2005, p.285).

She explains that 'each type of story holds out ideas, possibilities' (p.285) and describes how Paley 'discovered [that] play is the most effective curriculum for helping children practice and learn to think: to argue, debate, listen, negotiate, compromise, and to solve problems' (p.278).

In her books, Paley often provided 'detailed descriptions of how young children begin elementary school, building friendships and solving problems alongside one another through negotiating the dilemmas of heroes, heroines and their bad guys' (McNamee 2005, p.278), with children looking 'at one another with one thought in mind: "What role will you play in the unfolding story we can create together?"' (p.277). This play causes them to enter into a state of flow that results in 'a feeling of togetherness and friendship with a consequent loss of self-centredness' (Ellyatt 2010, p.91). Brennan says that:

> In bringing their stories together, children collectively construct an adapted story that continuously redefines who they are. As they compose their stories, children consider questions like, 'Do your actions belong in the scene you enter? If not, can you convince the players to alter the script or, failing to do that, will you agree to a different role?' (2008, p.262)

Paley (1990) says that this playing-your-part 'acceptably well in the given script' (p.37) *is* socialization and that this 'collaboration stimulates children to explain, share observations, engage in dialogue, combine strategies, exercise patience and complete tasks'. In fact, as the children 'push deeply into the collective imagination, it is easier' for them to 'establish connections and build mythologies' (Paley 1990, p.5), and also to expand their stories. As Paley says, 'An idea must find the rhythm of a group to be fully communicated. The imagination is not a unilateral function; it thrives in the company of those who share its point of view and ask the right questions' (Paley 1990, p.34). Just think of the adaptation of a book into a screenplay. We often marvel at a single person's interpretation of a story as we watch works that have been brought to life in the theatre or on the screen.

And this is essentially what happens as children co-operate in fantasy play. They create a sort of screenplay, allowing others to be a part of the extension and enhancement of their ideas. Paley, discussing the children's creation of stories, says that in 'the telling and performing of stories, all ideas must be heard, considered, compared, interpreted and acted upon' (1990, p.35). This co-operation, these interactions, cause the children to make new connections and to form new ways of thinking. McNamee says that this

> uniquely human capacity for play, to pretend, to suspend thought in the immediate here-and-now for the sake of discussing possibilities through socially constructed and elaborated scenarios, is the potential for intellectual growth the children offer each other and the teacher as they enter the classroom. (2005, p.277)

Sieving the story

'The narrative form…plays a key part in the development of children's capacity to make sense of events in their lives' (Smith *et al.* 2003, p.359) and is done through the engagement of their feelings and the exploration of them, particularly the more complicated ones (Burke 2012, p.1).

This extraction of deeper meaning can be compared to a sieving process. To sieve is to examine contents in detail. This is what occurs as children play, act, sing and pretend. The 'rich social interactions… provide opportunities for both rehearsals and re-enactments of roles and experiences' (Burke 2012, p.1), and children filter information, retaining what is essential and discarding what is superfluous. As they synthesize reworked versions of stories or create them anew, they are engaging in processes that research has shown to be 'valuable' in terms of 'the sharing of information, in negotiating meaning when conflicts arise with others' (Sydik 2016, p.15). Burke in fact refers to children as '"meaning makers" in their own lives' (p.1).

Part of this process consists of children asking questions. And it's essential that their questions are carefully considered, and that we encourage them to listen to one another as the questions are posed among peers.

> Listening to children's questions, taking them seriously and appreciating their taste for creative thought demand a lot of us…as we live in a time where creative thought, production of sense, invention and construction

of questions and problems are considered an absolute waste of time. (Olsson 2013, p.231)

Not only do children demand a lot of us as adults, but Paley (1990, p.10) says that as they engage in the composition of stories, they demand 'of one another intense concentration, contemplation, comparison, interpretation and self-evaluation'. She explains that 'children, at all ages, expect fantasy to generate – indeed they cannot stop it from doing so – an ongoing dialogue to which they bring a broad range of intellectual and emotional knowledge' (p.10). And their quest in all of it is meaning.

Story play and the discussion and reflection it fosters can, at times, raise questions and/or feelings of discomfort for parents and practitioners. One area that requires some attention in terms of sieving stories for meaning is children's focus on what can be considered as 'dark themes' in their play. We touched on the subject of darkness in children's literature previously, as discussed by the author Matt de la Peña about his book *Love* (2018).

Jeremy Sydik (2016), in his paper 'Hey, Where's the Monster? How a Storytelling Game Is Played in a Preschool Classroom', says that current culture promotes the 'viewpoint that children's stories, media, and games should avoid dark themes entirely' (p.75). However, he argues that 'this approach would seem to diminish the richness of experience that children bring to their understandings of the world as well as possibly deprive them of valuable tools in working cognitively through real concerns in their lives' (p.75).

It might seem strange to consider children's play and stories as pointing to the real world and real concerns, especially when this story and play is seemingly dark and random. But Gottschall (2013) cites Brian Sutton-Smith, who writes about the typical actions in young children's expressed stories as including events such as, 'being lost, being stolen, being bitten, dying, being stepped on, being angry, calling the police, running away or falling down' (p.34). Sutton-Smith explains that children's stories indeed 'portray a world of great flux, anarchy and disaster' (ibid.). Gottschall says that children's pretend play is about many things but is 'often about only one thing: trouble', and that often this 'trouble is existential' (p.33). Paley (1988, p.6), explains children's story play saying that 'the themes are vast and wondrous. Images of good and evil, birth and death, parent and child, move in and out of the real and the pretend. There is no small talk.' She sums up story play as 'a virtual recapitulation of life's enigmas' (p.32).

The author Maurice Sendak felt that children had the ability to handle stories that were dark and complicated (Fassler 2012) and it's reported that he was zealous about trying to draw what he felt was the way children, in reality, feel. Fassler (2012) says that 'children are unavoidably beset by grief, yearning, anxiety, and rage, the same wild and turbulent emotions that seize adult human beings'; and Sendak believed that their vulnerability to these emotions could lead to the perception of them as threatening. However, his conviction was that through fantasy they could begin to work through these difficult feelings, thereby acquiring a type of purging and a resulting sense of relief.

This issue of dark themes arouses strong feelings in parents and practitioners, with one persuasion being that childhood is a joyful, idyllic period where children must be shielded from adversity at all costs. But a different belief is that childhood can, at times, be 'disorienting, frightening and strange' (Fassler 2011) for children. Some 'psychologists, child specialists, and literary critics…argue that stories allow children to tame threatening feelings that might otherwise overwhelm them' (Fassler 2012), with child psychologist Bruno Bettelheim suggesting 'that fairy tales help children externalize, and ultimately diffuse, their deepest anxieties' (ibid.). As Fassler (2011) says, literature can teach children 'to cope, not cower'.

An example of the use of dark stories can be found in the Inuit culture. In an article titled 'How Inuit Parents Teach Kids to Control Their Anger', Doucleff and Greenhalgh (2019) discuss the Inuits' strong opposition to the idea of scolding, yelling at or punishing small children, relying rather on the use of stories to warn children of danger and to discipline them, aiming for behaviour modification. They, in fact, believe that these relatively hard-hitting stories can even save the children's lives.

One such story is a tale featuring a sea monster with a giant pouch on its back where it puts children who are found walking too close to the water's edge. It drags the children down to the bottom of the ocean where they are adopted out to a different family. Another short tale told by Inuit parents is about long fingers reaching out and grabbing children should they forget to ask before taking food. And there's another about the Northern Lights taking children's heads off and using them as a football, if children forget to wear their hats.

One of the authors writes about how the stories initially seemed to her to be a bit too frightening for young children and she therefore dismissed them. However, she quotes psychologist Deena Weisberg at Villanova University, who explains that 'stories with a dash of danger pull in kids like magnets', turning 'a tension-ridden activity like disciplining into a playful interaction'. Weisberg explains that 'with stories, kids get to see stuff happen that doesn't really happen in real life. Kids think that's fun' (Doucleff and Greenhalgh 2019).

The Inuit people demonstrated another useful parenting hack. When children in the camp acted out in anger or had a tantrum, parents would wait for the child to calm down before putting on a drama of their own. 'In a nutshell, parents would act out [in a playful way that involved the child], what happened when the child misbehaved, including the real-life consequences of that behavior' (Doucleff and Greenhalgh 2019), causing them to think through their actions. For example, if a child was hitting others, the mum would ask them to hit her instead. The child would have to consider whether to do this or not. If the child did hit, the mum would act out the consequences of being physically hurt or upset, exclaiming 'Ow, that hurts!' or asking a question such as 'Don't you like me?', communicating to the child the hurt experienced on both a physical and emotional level. Each time the child behaved in this particular manner the parent would repeat the drama until the behaviour stopped. This practice is deemed effective because children are able to practise different emotional reactions when not in the heat of the moment, the drama is carried out in a playful manner and humour underpins the interactions.

This ties in with Maurice Sendak's view of emotions in childhood: that children are not somehow shielded from them; that they, indeed, feel them. And that these emotions need to be recognized by the child (if not others), acknowledged through story (if not by others), tackled and sometimes resolved. Children love fantasy and fiction. They very often do not shy away from difficult subjects and complicated emotions in their quest to understand life and its meaning. We cannot always communicate meaning to children explicitly and when we do so, we rob them of the experience of finding it for themselves and making it their own. Children, very often, do not shy away from the exploration of difficult subjects and the resulting emotions. We therefore need to allow them to practise the feeling of them.

And they will do the work, with gentle support from us which bids us to 'first listen, and then contribute to the rhythms of their thinking with story, rhyme, folk tale and conversation that contribute to the transformation' of their thinking (McNamee 2005, p.287).

What does require awareness and reflection on our part is whether certain resources cause us, as adults to feel uncomfortable and challenged which results in the removal of such materials from the children. Fassler (2011) says that 'children seek out challenging experiences in books – because their anxieties are safer, smaller, and more manageable on the page'. If we censor the available resources due to feelings of discomfort, we can possibly deprive them of opportunities for growth.

Not all meaning is dark, serious and painful. Some is wonderful, joyful and beautiful. All of it, for children, is revelatory. As they engage in living and sieving the story, let's step back and allow them to do so soulfully, being present to answer questions wisely and unobtrusively, allowing them to truly lay claim to their carefully extracted meaning.

Giving the story

For me the questions are: How can each day's priorities and attachments be used to further an environment in which children tell us what they think? And what happens to those who remain on the outside?

Vivian Gussin Paley (1991, p.11)

We talk about expression or voice and we see this as, perhaps, a singular aspect of story where the child tells a story they've created, reads a poem they've written, performs a drama, dances or sings as the final act of the storytelling process. Expression does not, however, form or happen only at the final stages of the story process. It begins to develop when we engage in 'possibility thinking' (Craft n.d.) with the children, allowing them to make choices, and considering what exactly it is they're saying with their movements, games (McTavish 2006) and unique contributions.

Research work in a small number of classrooms in England with children aged 3 to 7 years (Craft n.d., citing Burnard, Craft and Grainger 2006; Cremin *et al.* 2006) investigated the pedagogic practices of staff and the children's learning, highlighting the significance of the *enabling context* where 'adults intentionally valued children's "agency", that is, children's abilities to have ideas and see these through into actions' (Craft n.d.).

An enabling context was seen to encourage children's motivation. Indeed, the degree to which the environment encourages agency is the degree to which the children will be imaginative, bold and expressive. Sunderland (2000, p.58), writing about how to respond effectively to stories says that the energy of the child is where the child's fascination is, and that our interference costs them a great deal:

> You may think you are being helpful, educative and supportive by giving the child new directions for his story. Yet, in fact, you may be quietly suffocating the child's own meaning, his sense of what is of central importance in his story... If you watch a child enacting something through story in the presence of a directive adult...an adult who offers 'adult-led' as opposed to 'child-led' play – you will often see the child's interest and aliveness fading before your eyes. He stops telling his story and moves on to something else... The images and characters in his story are robbed of the meaning he has given them. Now that his images and characters are imbued with the adult's meaning, they are useless to him.

We need to maintain an awareness of the dynamism of story: an awareness that throughout the entire process of crafting and telling, children are involved in the owning of information and ideas - sorting it all, reflecting on it all and refining it all. In this way, they 'can be recognized as experts and agents in their own lives' (Burke 2012).

Children express their stories in many different ways, in 'the hundred languages of children' which are 'expressive, communicative, symbolic, cognitive, ethical, metaphorical, logical, imaginative and relational' (Reggio Emilia Australia Information Exchange 2018). And as they express themselves in these many different ways, we should use a range of different methods to truly listen, as this recognition of various means of communication enables the richness of children's meaning-making to be shared with us (Wells 1999, cited by Burke 2012, p.1).

When we turn towards children and attune, when we focus and pay attention to their detail, our expressed sense of wonder at their creative endeavours will communicate to them that:

- they have worth

- they have a unique perspective to communicate

- their story is valid.

The actress Viola Davis, interviewed by the author Brené Brown and discussing her family history – and her father in particular – said something that really stayed with me. She said that there's

> an unspoken message that the only stories worth telling are the stories that end up in history books. This is not true. Every story matters. My father's story matters. We are all worthy of telling our stories and having them heard. We all need to be seen and honored in the same way that we all need to breathe. (Brown 2018)

This need was observed in an interesting project carried out by teachers at a school in California called Oak Knoll Elementary. The teachers made a decision to have their students keep notebooks, not for grading but rather as 'a place of private, free expression' (Schwartz 2013). One of the teachers, Karen Clancy, explained that the children were unused to being allowed to express themselves freely, about topics of their own choosing. However, once her students came to realize 'that they really weren't being graded and that they had freedom of expression, they eventually came to demand time to write' (Schwartz 2013). The children reportedly began to 'write and draw [about] what matters in their own lives', in the process developing 'their voice, humor, and point of view'. Andrea Boatright, another teacher using this approach (a resource now known as Lifebooks) commented on this increase in the children's agency saying, 'You have no power when you are a kid, but when you are telling stories you have incredible power' (Schwartz 2013).

Through the giving of stories to others, children can further reflect, affirm, adapt or even negate their perspectives. And this is often done in response to the observations and reactions of others. Our replies to their offerings must be enthusiastic if they are to be empowering. Indeed, if we truly wish for children to gain a sense of mastery over their own lives, we must love the sound of their voices as they speak their stories.

McNamee (2005) writes about how:

> Paley's classroom first and foremost stands as a place where every child is told in effect: this is a place where people gather who want to know you, understand your ideas and your point of view on questions raised in the group. Your stories – in play and conversation – are what count. All else important in school, and life, will follow. (p.286)

When we truly take this to heart as families and educators, when we listen for and to children communicating in every interaction that their stories matter – they will amaze us as they give us their treasured gifts of story.

Chapter 10

Story and Play

HELEN GARNETT

We have learned that, as humans, we are wired for storytelling. Stories captivate us. From the moment a favourite book is opened, children become active and alert, eyes grow round with attentiveness and little bodies are stock-still with expectation.

Listening to stories activates parts of the brain, such that the olfactory cortex lights up when a book describes the smell of roasting coffee and the motor cortex responds when a character in a book jumps or runs. Storytelling effectively synchronizes brains, where both storyteller and listener exhibit shared response patterns (Stephens, Silbert and Hasson 2010). This 'coupling' of brain response fades away altogether when communication is lost, demonstrating how significant the storytelling connection is.

What other behaviours occur during story time? Due to the attention commanded by an engaging story, children begin to listen, becoming immersed in the details of the narrative or text. They are highly observant, with their thoughts focused on the plot. Oxytocin, a neurochemical produced in the hypothalamus, may even be released when a story is particularly captivating, with its infusion leading to an increase in social behaviour (Zak 2015).

Indeed, for children, stories act as a springboard for exploration and social activity. They see stories as infinitely 'playful'. And they are right. Stories are play. Fantasy or make-believe and stories go hand in hand. 'You be Mummy and I'll be the baby' is a one-line story. Where the story goes from here is immaterial at this starting point. There does not have to be a neat and tidy beginning, middle and end. There simply needs to be a creative process; a stepping over into the imaginative, a brief suspension of reality.

And that's where the adult steps in. For if stories create such powerful connections, what happens when we are intentional about incorporating stories into children's play?

MAKING STORY CENTRAL

In many settings books are placed in a 'book corner'. This area is usually considered to be quiet, one where children passively engage in leafing through books or reading stories with little or no action on their part. However, books can and should become part of a child's everyday play world rather than being relegated to a certain area like the book corner. When we bring narrative into the heart of their play, children become story crafters and storytellers. Not only do they see or read the story, they are able to experience and live the story, and can also reinterpret and retell it. Using story in an active way enables them to live in a whole new landscape of imagination and play.

As children live and tell stories, their imagination is stirred, their curiosity fostered and complex emotional and cognitive processes are employed. A culture of inquiry and thinking supports these crucial cognitive processes. Children already have rich resources of understanding of stories, namely their working theories, as they theorize about their own unique world of favourite books and stories. In a climate of reciprocity, adults and children can immerse themselves in sustained shared inquiry and thinking. Adults can support children to use their existing understanding to build new, fresh understanding of both familiar and new stories. Every inquiry informs the children's next level of understanding, with this understanding enriched by 'real' questions and 'real' issues with a 'real' goal. As children and adults come together in this type of intense participation in stories, children can become inventive, resourceful and collaborative in their learning. And they can become accomplished storytellers, however simple their starting narratives.

SEEING STORY AS VITAL TO LEARNING

When we recognize storytelling as one of a child's primary needs rather than a learning outcome, we can effectively support children's narrative in play. You will have read about the idea of 'living the story' in Chapter 9. I'd like to expand on it a little more in a practical sense here.

Imagine a setting where the books stay firmly in the book corner: a 'Please put the book back neatly in the box' approach. What does this communicate to children about books and stories? If we are honest with ourselves, this is the practice in most of our settings, where books are used to calm and to quiet. Our culture around storytelling or story time communicates the idea that books are to be shared quietly and respectfully, usually in a carefully designated area or at a designated time such as circle time: that they are not to be carried around, delved into or opened up in other parts of the setting. This practice promotes the idea that books are for reading, not for playing with, and instils this belief in the children's attitudes.

I'm certainly not advocating for books to be carelessly treated or damaged in our enthusiasm to play with them, but we must be aware that books used only in the context of reading quietly alone, or in a group, are not being utilized to their full potential. Books contain rich stories and, within them, opportunities for exploration of virtues and character attributes, language, culture, creativity and humour. We therefore have to take books into children's play with boldness! Through play, children will enter into ever deepening levels of engagement with stories, considering them in a variety of different ways. We can provide space for children to set scenes, be characters, contemplate different outcomes – play, play, play out what they hear and see and absorb. Let the children transport the stories and the books they know and love into their play areas and begin to live the stories!

HOW DO WE FACILITATE THIS STORY PLAY?

Children's books generally have a set structure and we read them page by page, beginning to end. In order to 'live the story' we need to encourage children to be free with this chronology and to begin to engage with the narrative process through acts of creativity, imaginative play and resourceful thinking.

Let's take a look at different ways we can bring a book to life in the classroom on a practical level. We can:

- use the physical environment

- take risks and generate ideas through possibility thinking

- engage in collaborative thinking

- provide extended time and opportunity to explore.

A different book will be used as an example for each one of these categories to demonstrate how to enrich and extend children's narrative in play.

PROVIDE A PHYSICAL ENVIRONMENT THAT IS HIGHLY APPEALING AND ALLURING, USING *WE'RE GOING ON A BEAR HUNT* BY MICHAEL ROSEN

We're Going on a Bear Hunt requires a multisensory approach. When children have the opportunity to engage in learning using all of their senses, they deepen their understanding of the world around them. Swishy grass and squelchy mud beg for attention-grabbing sensory exploration. How do we provide this?

Mud kitchen

- Offer a range of different-sized and -shaped containers, tools and instruments to facilitate play.

- Allow the children to explore this medium freely, with aprons and boots on (if necessary) to protect clothing.

- Encourage exploration of the mud – touching, squeezing, immersing, lifting, splashing. Talk about 'squelchy' and 'squerchy'; does it make these sounds? Mix the mud, noticing the texture (slimy, wet, squidgy).

- Pin a picture of the relevant page at child height next to the kitchen to remind the children of the story.

- Notice created narratives and extend them, for example:

  – Child: 'My mud pies are ready to cook.'

– You: 'Let's get them in the oven ready for tea. Who's laid the table?'

Hay/straw play

- Provide 'swishy swashy' activities with hay/straw in a large container enriched with farm/zoo animals, tractors, lorries, wooden blocks, etc.

- Add chives/herbs for a distinctive smell.

- Encourage touching the grass; talk about 'swishy' and 'swashy'; sit quietly while you move the hay/straw. Is the sound description accurate? Note this together.

- Use fabric that 'swishes' to play with, e.g. scarves, flags – 'Oh, I can hear swishing. Can you?'

- Pin a picture of the relevant page at child height next to the hay/straw to remind children of the story.

- Notice narratives and extend them, for example:

  – Child: 'The trailer is carrying the hay to the farm.'

  – You: 'Oh, perfect! This lamb has a sore leg. Can he have a lift?'

Creative activities

- Offer 'swishy swashy' mark-making on large pieces of paper on the floor/easel/walls, using vibrant green markers/paint.

- Offer 'squelch squerch' mark-making using black/grey paint.

- Provide black/grey play dough.

- Notice narratives and extend them, for example:

  – Child: 'I've made a mud ball!'

  – You: 'Where is your mud ball going to roll?'

Obstacle courses

- Provide 'stumble trip' fun on intriguing obstacle courses through the inside and outside of the setting, e.g. jumping from chalk circle to chalk circle, walking through a 'forest' of traffic cones.

- Notice created narratives and extend them, for example:

  - Child: 'We are jumping!'

  - You: 'We are jumping like kangaroos in the grass!'

Water play

- Offer 'splash splosh' water activities – pouring, channelling, gathering water in a range of different-sized/shaped watering cans, buckets, cups, jugs, nets, funnels, boats, Small World ocean collection, etc.

- Notice created narratives and extend them, for example:

  - Child: 'I'll put this water in your bucket.'

  - You: 'You can pour it in like a waterfall.'

Ice play

- Offer 'hooo wooo' play with ice cubes in a water tray, with a range of different-sized/shaped spoons, Small World ocean collection, shells, adding food colouring for further enhancement.

- Notice created narratives and extend them, for example:

  - Child: 'The ice makes my hands cold.'

  - You: 'The ice is cold like snow.'

TAKE RISKS AND GENERATE IDEAS THROUGH POSSIBILITY THINKING, USING *THE GRUFFALO* BY JULIA DONALDSON

Children are at their most creative when they are given real and purposeful options and choices. Such options and choices are not just about whether to use sticky tape or glue. We need options in our thinking. Possibility thinking is about a child shifting from the simple understanding of what something is, to what they could do with it. Confident, creative decision makers are built when possibility thinking is used as the standard operating procedure in a setting. How do we generate this type of thinking?

Model curiosity

- Talk about what might happen next in stories during shared reading: 'Oh, no, here comes the Gruffalo. What do you think is going to happen?', 'I wonder if the mouse likes Gruffalo on toast?'

- Talk about what might happen next in children's play: 'I wonder what your tractor is going to carry next?'

- Notice created narratives and extend; model curiosity, for example:

  - Child: (Giving you a carrot) 'This is for your dinner.'

  - You: 'My favourite! I wonder what else I am getting for my dinner. What is on the menu?'

Take 'risks' in play

- Talk about events/actions that contain uncertainty: 'How can we build a forest?', 'How would we make Gruffalo crumble?' Encourage the children to 'have a go': 'Let's try to make one. What do we need first?'

- Notice created narratives and extend; model taking risks, for example:

- Child: (Playing with cars on mat) 'Brrrmmm. I'm going to the park.'

- You: 'Let's take the cars to the forest. We might meet the Gruffalo!'

Immerse the children in creative activities and choices

- Make dens using fabric; build caves out of wooden crates; make a 'river'; go for a bug/bear/mouse hunt, etc.

- Model-making choices: 'Shall we use this blue fabric or this red one?'

- Notice created narratives and extend, for example:

  - Child: 'Get in the house everyone!'

  - You: 'Everyone get in the house. We need to listen out for the Gruffalo!'

Question and investigate together

- Ask questions during play: 'What if...?', 'How...?', 'What will happen if we...?'

- Model investigating: 'Let's go and find out where the best fabric is to make our den', 'Let's build it higher. How could we do that?'

- Notice created narratives; model questioning and investigating, for example:

  - Child: 'My den is big.'

  - You: 'How did you make it so tall? Let's find out!'

Note: It is the choices in these processes that build the decision maker. When children become decision makers, they decide where/what to explore, and how to explore it. With support and a degree of success in their explorations, their confidence soars.

ENCOURAGE COLLABORATIVE STORYTELLING, USING *THE VERY HUNGRY CATERPILLAR* BY ERIC CARLE

Stories are by their very nature collaborative. We read and enjoy them together. We experience a sense of wonder together. In the same way, play can be highly collaborative. When we combine the two together, we create a type of collaborative play, a dance of exploration, where learning is communal and where the collective culture of the group can be shared and celebrated.

Collaborative storytellers are highly effective narrators. One idea bounces off the next: 'You be Mummy; let's go to the park', 'I'll take the picnic; you make the cake.' Already here we have a context, characters and some objects. A story is born, and children can begin to combine their thoughts and ideas, presenting them to each other, creating a continuous narrative throughout their play. Collaborative play encourages the timid child to become a storyteller, and the more assertive child to become a story listener. The beauty of story is that any child can be involved as teller or listener, without learning to read or write.

How do we encourage collaborative storytelling?

- Read favourite stories over and over: carefully observe the favourite stories of the children and read them time and time again, even in the same sitting. Take the same book to read under a tree in the garden, inside a den or under a table. Children love the pleasure of the unexpected; it teaches them that the uncertain can be made safe and enjoyable.

- Provide richly resourced role-play areas: offer appealing props to support role-play, e.g. real fruit, real leaves and objects from nature, cooking and baking equipment, real household items.

- Provide resources that encourage collaboration, e.g. mixing smoothies, making fruit salads together, raising real caterpillars to grow into butterflies, plenty of cooking utensils, large wooden building blocks.

- Notice created narratives; model questioning and investigating, for example:

  - Child: 'I like apples.'

  - You: 'I like apples and bananas and grapes! What other fruits do you like? We like some of the same things and some different things!'

OFFER EXTENDED TIME AND OPPORTUNITY TO PLAY AND EXPLORE, USING *RAINBOW FISH* BY MARCUS PFISTER

The process of play has no objectives other than the process. This is what makes it so appealing. It is random, creative and beautiful. It is the process that rewards, not the outcome.

Arts and crafts can seem like the obvious place to explore or extend our understanding of a book in preschool. While this is a good start, there are far more ways to 'live a story' than by painting, cutting and sticking. Every area of the early years' curriculum has a place for narrative. Mathematics and science are key areas where communicative language is central. Likewise, movement, drama and music are highly communicative and interactional. Placing stories intentionally into distinct areas builds vital vocabulary specific to that particular area of learning.

The time allowed for such activities is key to the children's enjoyment and investigative potential. If we are not careful, a rigid 'put the toys away' timetable can break up the creative process and enthusiasm. The luxury of time must be afforded. In this way children can pretend, investigate and explore to their heart's content. And in this type of intentional creative environment, ideas can grow and mature. This is creativity at its most resourceful and energizing.

How do we do this?

- *Make up stories together*: Offer role-play filled with appealing props, for example, rainbow-coloured scarves to drape or water play with Small World ocean play. As the children play, model making up stories: 'Once upon a time, there was a little fish who didn't like water!' Accept the children's contributions with enthusiasm and joy. Elaborate further: 'Oh wait, are fish able to live outside of water?' Investigate and explore together.

- *Mix paints together to create the colours of the Rainbow Fishes' scales*: Offer different coloured paints in a large container, combining two colours to make a third colour. Discuss what happens when we mix paints; discuss shades and intensity of colour; discuss personal colour preferences; discuss how colours can make us feel.

- *Talk about the characters we meet in books*: Decide which fish we like, and which we don't; which fish we want to be like; which ones scare us, anger us, excite us, motivate us.

- *Notice the child's created narrative in play*: When we notice narrative in everyday play, we can extend it, for example:

  - Child: 'My fish is eating.'

  - You: 'Your fish is so hungry. He hasn't had his breakfast. That may make him feel grumpy.'

FACTORS AFFECTING CHILDREN'S RESPONSE TO NARRATIVE
Conation

Stories and play in tandem will be most effective and inspiring when children are fully and genuinely engaged in their play. Motivation is key.

Children are naturally curious. They are already motivated to learn through conation. 'What is conation?', you might ask. Conation is the stronger, bigger sister to motivation. It is the inner drive to learn, the determination behind the engagement. A toddler learns to walk because there is an inner drive to do so. The same conation will urge a child to learn to talk, run or ride a bike.

Conation can drop when a child loses their drive to learn through discouragement. Discouragement is a process where there is a hindrance or interference, in this instance, in the child's play. Discouragement can take the form of negative words, a rigid timetable, a physical environment that is uninviting and unrewarding, or the interference of a well-meaning practitioner who upsets the child's sense of autonomy and agency.

Conation is crucial in inspiring early learning. Reliable and dedicated adults support conation, giving children room to create, to invent and reinvent, to reflect and to extract meaning, without projecting or injecting their own ideas into the play in a way that would hijack it. There is significant power in making room for conation as it produces higher-level brain action (Huitt and Cain 2005) and throughout life is crucial in the understanding of one's own aspirations, intentions and goals. It is one of the proactive aspects of our behaviour.

Through the understanding and facilitation of this motivating force, children are equipped to explore and investigate their environment with confidence.

Culture and shared identity

Where else do we see culture more clearly than in stories? Culture groups people together. These groups are created due to a shared identity, and this is based on communal customs, values, priorities and beliefs, along with other factors such as routines, food and clothes. Culture plays a crucial role in establishing our personal identity. Where we come from influences who we will become. Identity is about belonging. Even if we may not 'like' our culture, it gives us a starting point, and helps us to form a sense of self and a sense of others.

Books are essentially all about culture, from *The Gruffalo* to *Rainbow Fish*. These books provide an immediate understanding of another culture. *The Gruffalo* sees us in a forest 'culture', with a difficult character – the Gruffalo – determined to frighten the life out of all the other characters. The brave mouse outwits the Gruffalo and, in the end, bravery wins the day. The culture is one of support, shared identity and fighting against the enemy. These are complex concepts but can be understood in a shared reading context. In *Rainbow Fish*, where identity is caught up in the appearance of 'beautiful, shining scales' the Rainbow Fish learns about true happiness. He accepts the wisdom of the Octopus and discovers that the more he gives away his shiny scales the happier he becomes. This is a powerful story of discovery, where the culture of kindness is strong and the culture of change – and the ability to learn and to do so – is highlighted.

In short, stories support the introduction to, and exploration and acceptance of, one's own culture and those of others, leading to a healthy sense of identity and huge scope for understanding others.

Making connections

How many times have you read a book to children, and they say, 'I know this one!' Children love connections. They love connections that are expected, and ones that are not. Making a connection is one of the rewards of exploration. 'I know this!' helps children to engage further because they recognize that there is a purpose to the process, that they can extend what they already know to acquire new information and that they can then know this too!

Children are able to make connections more easily when adults become true storytelling/listening play partners. Co-constructing activities, that is, constructing story/play activities with the child, has an effect on a child's learning because it deepens their engagement and 'quickens' their learning.

What environments best support children making connections?

- *Multisensory environments*: A real orange to touch and taste is infinitely more satisfactory than a 2D picture of an orange. When-ever possible we need to offer real objects rather than plastic versions. This gives a distinctive and powerful purpose to the child's play.

- *Thinking environments*: When adults visibly 'think' about what is happening and what it is they are doing, children's thinking skills are strengthened. Adults can support children best by sourcing appropriate books that lend themselves to the children's interests and passions, and taking the learning 'off the page' by making real life, relevant connections to the child's existing knowledge and understanding, and modelling this for them, e.g. 'I think that you have a car like this at home?'

- *Following children's interests*: Children's 'working theories' (their present understanding of any concept/object/thing and how it connects to their immediate/outer world) need exploration and investigation. This means that children need to touch, taste, hear, lift, push, pull, drop, etc. The more they do this, the more connections they make. Adults support this process by narrating what the child is doing/learning: 'I remember that you like playing with this green tractor. What is the tractor carrying today?', 'You've found a beetle. Let's find it somewhere dark to sleep because beetles...'

Adult cues

An adult's understanding of the child's needs and playful responses underpins the child's creativity. Creativity is cultivated when adults support play, rather than impose on it. Creativity is the by-product of all co-constructed play-based curriculum/activities. Choice and creativity are excellent play partners. Interactions that are based on shared understanding and collective control will extend playfulness and thereby maximize learning.

The crucial point is that children work out what is playful and what is 'work' according to our cues. As a result their 'performance' is affected. Generally speaking those children who choose a task sitting on the floor, or in a playful stance, display more learning and engagement but less distraction than a child who has no choice, and is sitting at a table with an adult.

Children who attend a setting where activities are co-constructed, and where adults are present or nearby to offer gentle support, will be attracted to a greater range of play activities, not seeing some of them as 'playful' and others as 'work' but rather all as playful.

WHERE DOES THIS TAKE US WITH STORIES AND PLAY?

- Adults need to mindfully choose stories with positive themes that children can play out and use as a springboard for further activities.

- Adults need to co-construct stories alongside the children, keeping these playful.

- Adults need to know when to step aside, allowing the children choice and control over their new stories: too much attention, and practitioners become overbearing; too little and the children are unsupported. This is a delicate balance to achieve but, once mastered, leads to increased creativity on the part of the child.

THEORY OF MIND

Part of understanding children's needs is an awareness of the suitability of stories in terms of their developmental level. Very young children have not yet developed Theory of Mind (ToM), which is the understanding that other people's thinking is different to theirs. This will affect how they view stories and books.

Adults need to be aware that those children who have not yet developed ToM need books that are action oriented whereas children who have developed ToM (for example older preschoolers) require books that are more consciousness oriented, that is they reveal the inner world of the characters. Books where action and consciousness are integrated, such as *Rainbow Fish* are suitable for use with both groups of children as they allow for a focus on drawing out the consciousness-based elements of the book for those able to understand, while beginning to guide the children who are still developing their ToM.

Shared reading supports the development of ToM, because being around children of a similar age with different thoughts facilitates children's commentary and discussion, broadening the collaborative thought process while teaching and guiding the less-developed children.

CONCLUSION

Narrative competence, which is the ability to understand and make up stories, develops in the preschool years. It begins at a very basic story level ('My teddy sad'), building detail and texture as the child matures, and develops ToM ('My teddy is sad because his mummy has gone away'). Story is the most natural form of communication for young children. When we fully understand the extraordinary aptitude that children have to think in story and communicate in metaphor, only then can we fully support it. As Albert Einstein said, 'If you want your children to be intelligent, read them fairy tales. If you want them to be very intelligent, read them more fairy tales' (Winick 2013). I would add to this: 'If you want your children to be creative, explore and live the stories you share together. If you want them to be even more creative, live the stories all over again!'

And we can join them on their journey of exploration in terms of their immediate world, their interests and their flights of fancy. We can allow them to be the 'expert' in the context of their stories and their play.

When we practise this daily, we build confident storytellers and competent listeners who feel that their voices are heard and valued and who, in turn, listen to and value the stories of others.

Our communication skills depend on our ability to listen to and tell stories. We communicate using stories every day, in every situation, with every person we meet. Being intentional about building narrative competence and story appreciation in children's play will place them at a huge advantage, giving them the ability to communicate more effectively and to connect with others successfully throughout their lives. This is the powerful influence of story when placed at the heart of play.

Chapter 11

Story

Towards a Lifelong Love of Learning

At the beginning of the novel *The Librarian of Auschwitz* (Iturbe 2019), a book based on the life story of Dita Kraus, a teenage prisoner in what was known as the 'family camp' at Auschwitz-Birkenau, the author describes how everything that pertains to schooling and education was forbidden. But there is one character in the story who continues to teach the children and to oversee the guarding of the few books in the prisoners' possession which are deemed valuable beyond measure. Iturbe describes the character thus:

> He was always smiling enigmatically, as if he knew something that no one else did. 'It doesn't matter how many schools the Nazis close', he would say to them. 'Each time someone stops to tell a story and children listen a school has been established.' (Iturbe 2019, p.1)

Throughout this book we've considered story in terms of early development. We know that children are learning through story from birth but can this same device continue to be useful as children grow and learn what is deemed to be 'properly', as they move from their earliest years to the formal study of literacy, numeracy and STEM (science, technology, engineering, maths) subjects? What would this learning even look like? With an overarching question to consider, which is 'What does it mean, ultimately, to be educated?' And can we say – with confidence – that we're currently headed in the right direction? I would suggest that, without a focus on story as a key part of all learning processes, we are not.

In a 2016 interview on raising brilliant kids, the developmental psychologist Kathy Hirsh-Pasek discussed 'the "six Cs"…collaboration, communication, content, critical thinking, creative innovation and confidence'. Hirsh-Pasek believes that it is these factors that will enable children to achieve what she calls 'the 21st century view of success' which she describes as 'a happy, healthy, caring child who grows up to be a collaborative person, a creative innovator, a thinking person and a social person, while also being a good citizen' (Turner and Kamenetz 2019).

It is crucial, I believe, for us to consider our systems of education in light of Hirsh-Pasek's statement above, and as we face rapidly changing times; to let go of traditional ideas and expectations, and to begin to understand the transmission of knowledge in a more integrated way.

'Time spent reading together creates a special, magical place', Taylor Monaco told Cox Gurdon (Cox Gurdon 2019, p.61). As we have discovered, learning does not begin when children enter school but is built on foundations established from birth. The sequential processes of reading and mathematics, the inquiry of science, and the curiosity and creative thinking necessary for academic endeavour are established in the earliest years of life through secure attachment and close relationships, and through the bathing of children in the language of conversation, rhyme, song and story. It is in these rituals of reciprocity that children begin to understand the power of language as a tool of expression, a form of communication and a means by which to uncover knowledge. Reading a book together is as much about what are called '"serve and return" interactions (child-adult-child-adult) and "dialogic reading" (asking questions, letting the child help tell the story)' as it is about reading what is actually written on the page (Klass 2017). Literacy is not merely the ability to decode. It is a process that begins prior to reading and writing and continues on as we incorporate those abilities. Being literate is 'the product of a whole range of brain circuits from vocabulary and vision and visual processing to memory and meaning' (ibid.) and it includes our listening, our speech, our reading and our writing. We cannot view literacy as 'just one restricted developmental zone, one arbitrary hurdle' (ibid.). Instead we need to view it in its full glory: as an all-encompassing process involving the sourcing of interesting and appropriate stories that require an enthusiastic approach, sustained joint inquiry and attention, conversation, fun and socio-dramatic play. Indeed, 'many contemporary researchers into reading' argue that 'we need to build on this spontaneous creation' of constructed narrative through play 'if we are to sustain children's interest in actually reading stories for themselves' (Smith *et al.* 2003, p.359).

Research-based evidence, in fact, indicates that the strongest predictors of success in a child's learning life – and their literacy – are not the education, status or socio-economic background of their parent. Rather it has been shown to be something far more elemental.

STORYTELLING

Engel (2016) points to the findings of Wells (1986) who, in a study of children in Bristol, showed 'that those who told and heard stories at home under 4 years old were the most likely to have ease and interest in learning to read once they got to school'. This is because they have developed both oral language skills and 'narrative capacity' which 'form the foundation for reading comprehension, the ability to produce coherent writing, and the ability to understand subjects such as history, social studies, and science' (Bay Area Early Childhood Funders 2007).

Further evidence of the profound effect exposure to literature has on children can be found in a 20-year study led by Mariah Evans, an associate professor at the University of Nevada in Reno, United States. The study showed an equal effect on the level of education attained by a child due to the difference between being raised in a home with no books and being raised in a home with a library of five hundred books, and the difference between having parents who were barely literate and those who had a university education. The large library and degree-educated parents have been shown to 'propel a child 3.2 years further in education, on average' (University of Nevada 2010). Even the possession of a few books in the home has a 'significant impact on propelling a child to a higher level of education', with the more books added the greater the evidential benefits.

Unfortunately, what often transpires once children leave their early childhood education settings – and sadly, in some cases, beforehand – is a move away from the joy and wonder of story and the resulting play and exploration, and towards the technical aspects of phonics, reading and comprehension. This is where many children are alienated and some, sadly, lost.

The author Michael Morpurgo in a speech for the Book Trust explains his transition from a love of stories to a feeling of being cut off from them, saying:

> I had loved stories before I went to that school, because my mother read to us…her favourite stories and poems…with a passion. We loved them with a passion. They were fun, they were exciting, I longed for our storytime with her, loved books, loved stories. School killed all that, took the wonder of stories, the music and playfulness of language, and turned it all into a 'subject', to be used for comprehension tests, handwriting tests, grammar tests, parsing, spelling tests and punctuation tests. In these tests at least as many of us failed as succeeded… When you fail it brings only a sense of worthlessness and hopelessness. It brings fear and shame and anxiety…rocks confidence, ruins self-esteem. You disappoint yourself, disappoint others. You give up. I gave up. To give up on books is to give up on education, and if you give up on education, then you can so easily give up on hope, give up on your future. This way you can so easily turn children away from books and reading, and that can be a life sentence, a life without books. So many avenues are barred, so many possibilities never imagined, so many discoveries never made, so much understanding of yourself, of others, stunted forever. (Morpurgo 2017)

This description of being cut off from literacy should be a sobering warning to us all. Sue Palmer, the literacy specialist and author of *Toxic Childhood: How Modern Life Is Damaging Our Children and What We Can Do About It* (2010) and *Upstart: The Case for Raising the School Starting Age and Providing What the Under-Sevens Really Need* (2016), is passionate about raising awareness about the long-term damage that starting literacy instruction before the age of 7 does to young children. Indeed, research shows that there is no long-term advantage for this type of instruction 'but plenty of potential for long-term damage – physical, emotional, social and cognitive' (Palmer 2016). Palmer points to the European countries 'with the best record in terms of literacy' who 'provide play-based kindergarten education for the under-sevens, with plenty of time for stories and song as well as lots of opportunities for active, outdoor play', with children who show an interest in reading and writing supported at the level at which they're working.

As children playfully communicate their stories using modalities of their choice, this will lead to a desire to develop the skills of composing and decoding text. In a 2012 Community Playthings article, a practitioner writes about the connection between children's block play and literacy. She describes how children, after hearing a story, would head to the block play area to re-enact it with blocks, and how she realized what they were doing was in essence 'writing' their story, using their blocks as symbols to represent ideas (Community Products 2012a). She tells of one child who, using blocks, had rebuilt a map on the inside cover of his favourite book. When she asked the child's teacher whether he could have drawn the map using a pencil and paper, the teacher replied that the 'pinnacle' of his mark-making skills was the drawing of rainbows. The practitioner remarks on how this memorization of the map would have been missed had the child in question not had a medium through which he could express himself comfortably. He was not yet writing but he was 'fluent in the language of blocks'.

In another Community Playthings article on storytelling, a different practitioner writes about the use of only a small and a large cylinder to tell the story of Little Red Riding Hood to the children. He reports on how the children knew exactly which cylinder represented which person, and how all that was required to create a forest was a few tall blocks placed on end. He details how other elements of the story can be recreated with the blocks (e.g. a bed and a house), with the beauty being that 'children readily imagine detail, and the same block can be a bear, a bed, a car, or a boat. There is no limit to the number of stories you can tell with one set of blocks' (Community Products 2012b). Indeed, stories can be told with a collection of materials from nature like twigs and stones, or with loose parts in the home and classroom, constructed using Lego or played out with soft toys, dolls and action figures. The author Mo Willems, discussing drawing, says that it is 'a very accessible form of writing. Many writers use storyboards or make maps or sketches, even if they're only writing prose. There's an inherent value in drawing that's really powerful.' He explains that children tend to draw chronologically, which is to say narratively. They'll start with, 'Oh, I'm going to draw a character. Now, is it a hero or a villain? It's a villain. Well, if it's a villain, it has a cape. And if it has a cape, it can fly. Let me draw the sky.' And all of that story comes out of having a drawing utensil in your hand. It's magic. (In Kaplan 2020)

This expression of ideas in various concrete forms, and the move from the concrete (the dolls and figures) to the more abstract (the cylinders), prepares children for the symbolic representation of ideas in abstract form at a later stage. Due to its effectiveness, this story play should not be limited to the early years, with concrete representation aiding in terms of writing throughout life. McNamee, writing about Paley, says that the more Paley encouraged children's play over the years, 'the more articulate, creative and expressive the children became': and that Paley's collective works now 'show how her methodology of teaching through fostering pretend play' leads to 'highly educated children' (McNamee 2005, p.278).

Sir Ken Robinson (2010) describes education as 'a personal process', explaining that 'what and how young people are taught have to engage their energies, imaginations and their different ways of learning'. We need to understand that children do not see the world divided into different subjects with learning compartmentalized. Rather, they learn in a holistic manner with their learning becoming more meaningful as they make connections. In fact, their acquisition of knowledge moves in the opposite direction to standardized curricula, aiming always to join the dots. Isolating subjects the way we currently do 'can make it difficult for children to make both inter-subject links and feel the impact of these school subjects on their everyday lives' (Burke 2007, p.6). This unnatural way of learning is illustrated beautifully by Elvin (1977, p.29) who says, 'When you are out walking, nature does not confront you for three quarters of an hour only with flowers and in the next only with animals.' The author Michael Rosen (2017) explains the work of the academic and researcher Carol Fox, saying:

We need to remember that before children get to know that there are ways in which we chop up the world into 'subjects' like geography, chemistry or philosophy, each with their own way of describing and investigating the world, telling stories has to cover or include all these subjects and ways of thinking.

As we have learned, Paley placed dramatic play at the centre of learning, and in her practice she used subjects like science, maths and physical education only in the context of, and in support of, the stories being told by the children. She responded to children's curiosity and their ideas, listened closely to them and searched for connections. These natural processes gave birth to questions that connected 'Paley and the children to historical, mathematical, scientific, artistic, literary, social and moral issues every day of the year' (McNamee 2005, p.280). As Ellyatt (2010) says, 'Children seek out meaningful work' (p.93) and we can respond to this search as Paley did, harnessing these natural thinking processes – this motivation – by considering all topics in the light of story, aiming to weave the thread of narrative through our lessons. We can tell children the stories of scientists, mathematicians and engineers as we teach STEM subjects, adventurers as we teach geography and we can explore the complexities of people who feature prominently in history. This works because we are driven by our socially oriented design. As Will Storr writes in *The Science of Storytelling*, 'It's people, not events, that we're naturally interested in. It's the plight of specific, flawed and fascinating individuals' (2019, p.6). This people-lined pathway is how we ignite a passion for learning in the lives of the children we teach.

PRACTICAL EXAMPLES OF INTRODUCING A HUMAN ELEMENT TO LEARNING
Geography

- Start with a place: What happened there? Why is it relevant?

- Think about explorers – what they found; how they found it; their struggles, failures and achievements.

- Use geographical terms in a human context (e.g. eroded/ subsided); find poetry about nature.

- Talk about favourite places and draw or write about them, focusing on sensorial aspects.

- Think about land and resources in terms of human rights and responsibilities, in terms of equality and justice (this can be done from a very young age).

Science

- Who was Newton? Galileo? Einstein?

- What were their passions?

- What drove them?

- What were the issues of the day? What was popular opinion?

- What obstacles did they face and overcome?

- How do we use this science today? What is its effect on our daily lives, if any?

History

- What event happened? Who was born?

- What were the effects on people's lives then/now?

- Look at events through the eyes of conflicting players; research individual accounts of everyday people.

- Drill down to the human element that causes children to ask and reflect, 'What if that were me?'

When we introduce the human element, we establish relevance. 'Learners of all ages are more motivated when they can see the usefulness (relevance) of what they learn and its impact on their own lives' (Haven 2007, p.65, citing Bransford and Stein 1993; McCombs 1996, p.70; Pintrich and Schunk 2002). It is stories that provide 'tools, context, relevance, and elements readers need in order to understand, remember and index the beliefs, concepts and information in the story' (Haven 2007, p.71) because they are units 'that can be easily found, easily recalled and told' (p.69). He explains that 'we have great difficulty remembering abstract concepts and data. However, we can easily remember a good story' (p.71).

The more we provide children with opportunities to listen to and create stories, the more exposure they will have to extracting information from material that is meaningful and relevant, the stronger their conceptual understanding will be, the better the connections formed to build knowledge across the subject spectrum and the better their memory. This information should further cause us to weigh up our traditional approach to learning, which thus far 'has relied on the transmission, accumulation and reproduction of information' which can be likened to 'a long linear staircase that we must climb' (Ellyatt 2010, p.89). Rosen (2010) says that there is a prevailing presumption that learning happens according to a 'jug and mug theory of education' where the child is the empty mug and the teacher is the full jug, with the full jug tipped into the empty mug for the transference of knowledge. He explains that a 'huge body of theory and practice' show that this is not the way to understanding, particularly for young learners. Rather, Rosen says:

> In order to learn we need to be in a position in which we are open to receiving ideas, processes, sensations and feelings – the gamut of human experience; we need to have been allowed to respond to these experiences in ways that aren't inhibited through being told that this or that response is wrong or insufficient; we need to know that the response can come through thought, talk, action, activity, solo or collective; we need to have time and space to reflect on our responses – at least some of the time in cooperation with others. In these circumstances we will be creative in thought and action. We will advance in whichever field of human activity we can think of. (2010, foreword)

HOW DO WE BECOME INCREASINGLY STORY FOCUSED ON A PRACTICAL LEVEL?

How do we begin to place story at the centre of children's learning, particularly in light of systems that are static and burdensome in terms of outcomes, standards and workload? Is a move to more creative learning simply too much to ask of often already overworked practitioners and parents?

I believe that it is possible for us to begin to place story and dramatic play at the very core of our work because 'all areas of learning have the potential to be creative experiences' (Duffy 2010, p.21). Through the taking of simple steps and the making of small changes, practice at home and in school can be transformed.

Acknowledging children's 'knowing', that is, their 'rich ideas, questions, and skills for expressing themselves in play, drawing, movement, conversation, song, and block building' (McNamee 2005, p.285); and understanding that though their earliest stories may be simple and 'fragmentary', this communication will provide us with insight into their minds (Smith *et al.* 2003, p.359). Indeed, it is this respect for them as autonomous contributors that will enhance interactions and lead to greater degrees of connection and engagement.

Understanding that as we build children's narrative capacity, they will be established as writers and as readers, and beginning to view stories and the resulting discussion and play as the roots of learning rather than a deviation from it; having security in the knowledge that writing and reading 'float on a sea of talk' (Britton 1970, p.164).

Following the children's interests where we can so that they want to read about what they want to know and write about what they do know.

We can ensure that literacy is approached in a holistic manner, and that storytelling and dramatic play are featured prominently in early childhood teacher training. One suggestion is that 'during teacher training, the educator students should go through the same process of storytelling that they will implement later on with children: writing stories, creating storyboards, and illustrating, using supportive media if needed' (Istance and Paniagua 2019, p.33). The idea is for teachers to be proficient in all aspects of storytelling and elements of story structure. I would go further here, positing that teachers themselves need to play out stories, to compose them using concrete materials, to move from the concrete to the more abstract and to gain a full understanding of how dramatic play gives rise to story composition, the creation of story connections, the making of meaning and the motivation to hear and in turn create more stories.

Implementing creative systems of learning where possible. I

particularly like the 'four Ps of creative learning' devised by Mitchel Resnick (2019), Professor of Learning Research at the MIT Media Lab and author of the book *Lifelong Kindergarten: Cultivating Creativity through Projects, Passion, Peers, and Play* (2017). Resnick talks about how he and his team consider how they can 'provide children with opportunities to work on projects, based on their passions, in collaboration with peers, in a playful spirit' (Resnick 2019).

Let's consider each 'P' in further detail:

- *Projects*: Working on projects allows children to 'learn new skills in a meaningful and motivating context' (Resnick 2019) and to put their knowledge into practice. Work to create projects based on favourite books using the topics, characters and themes contained within. This can be done individually, in groups or as a whole school.

- *Passion*: When children work on things they care about, they're willing to work longer and harder. Passion gives rise to motivation and grows perseverance. Have children choose books that they're excited about and discuss them together, research further and find similar resources on the same subject or books written by the same author. New stories will give rise to new passions. The more stories children hear, the more interests and passions they will develop.

- *Peers*: Children gain new insight as they work together. Tom Hobson, discussing story and dramatic play in his former preschool in Seattle says that children tell 'stories to and with our friends, building upon one another's imaginations, negotiating, insisting, compromising, dreaming' (Hobson 2019).

  Create opportunities for children to talk about books together. Think about what the text is saying together, what each child feels, what each child thinks. Try not to be confined by the work of the author but open to combining the ideas of the author with those of the children. It is the marrying of the two that creates a new story life.

- *Play*: Resnick says that he likes to think of play, 'not as an activity, but as an attitude, a way of engaging with the world' (Resnick 2019). As we adopt a playful attitude, we can begin to approach the stories we tell and read and the writing tasks we set for children in a creative manner, allowing them to do the same. Make room for the children to draw out of stories the aspects they wish to explore and reinvent; have them hypothesize, deconstruct and reconstruct; use humour; and, where possible, visit realms of the impossible and fantastical with them.

It is stories that 'help children...cultivate imaginative and divergent thinking – that is, thinking that generates a range of possible ideas and/or solutions around story events' (Albers 2016). Try to remove fixed ideas, and to shake off the way-things-'should'-be-done approach that so many of us carry from our own childhoods. Rosen (2010) says, 'There needs to be a sense that there are many ways of getting things "right", rather than a simple binary of "right or wrong".' Tom Hobson, discussing a strict adherence to a right-and-wrong approach in terms of learning explains that the 'cult of right answers leads to classrooms in which authority figures guide their students through material towards a predetermined destination' and that children 'who have wonderful ideas along the way may be indulged for a time, but the goal is always to guide them back onto the only pathway that leads to right answers.' He goes further, saying that 'the having of wonderful ideas doesn't lead to right or wrong answers, but rather toward *new* ideas... When one has a wonderful idea, it compels pursuit, which leads to more new ideas, and more. The most wonderful ideas are those that in turn inspire wonderful ideas in others' (Hobson 2020).

This is the beauty of story and play – where children get to think and feel without fear, in total freedom, where they can be vulnerable in their innovation. The author Brené Brown, who researches shame and vulnerability, in her book *Daring Greatly: How the Courage to Be Vulnerable Transforms the Way We Live, Love, Parent, and Lead*, reports that:

> 85 percent of the men and women interviewed for the shame research could recall a school incident from their childhood

that was so shaming that it changed how they thought of themselves as learners. What makes this even more haunting is that approximately half of those recollections were what I refer to as creativity scars. The research participants could point to a specific incident where they were told or shown that they weren't good writers, artists, musicians, dancers, or something creative. This helps explain why the gremlins are so powerful when it comes to creativity and innovation. (Brown 2013, p.190)

Sharing stories of our own with children. Children love to hear anecdotes and stories about the personal experiences of the significant people in their lives because these stories help them to make sense of the world. As adults, we can bear in mind that children may benefit 'from hearing what you had to give up, who encouraged you, what you hope to accomplish, and it can be especially reassuring for them to hear that you did not always succeed and how you handled failures or near-failures' (Noddings n.d., p.10). This sharing has the power to strengthen bonds as it reveals the personhood of parents, teachers and caregivers. Children remember these stories, and they sometimes become part of the children's own. Of course, we need to share wisely and appropriately, taking care to tailor our stories to the children's ages, stages and needs.

Inviting visitors to share their stories with the children – not professional storytellers or authors necessarily – but everyday people who have everyday stories to share. This will affirm the idea that everybody's story is of equal value.

Understanding that story can be used with any child, anywhere. Stories can be simplified for children with additional needs and those accessing a certain language for the first time. They can be created sensorially, and specialist stories such as Social Stories™, developed by Carol Gray in 1990, are stories which can be used with individuals with autism to exchange information that is personalized and illustrated. Social Stories™ are usually short, simple and have defined criteria to make them 'Social Stories'. This is the beauty of story – the possibility it holds for simplification, adaptation and reinvention, for use with all learners, for extension and expansion.

Then, we can consider the stories we're telling about the children to ourselves and to others. Are we casting them as creators? As current or future readers and writers? Are we writing a positive story with the thoughts we think and the words we speak? Do our stories require editing in order to be ones of hope and potential where children are scripted as the competent contributors they can be?

And, last, we can acknowledge that changing practice and facilitating new ways of learning and being will not always be easy. Esme Ward of the Whitworth Gallery explains their changing approaches to learning, describing how, 'by promoting enquiry-based and child-led activity, by developing our role as facilitators rather than teachers or leaders, we are learning how to be more confident and comfortable with the uncertainty and ambiguity this approach necessarily entails' (Ward 2010). A more hands-off approach to learning can require some getting used to. It is often the norm to decide for children and to direct them – even in their play – as we are driven by our tasks and detailed objectives rather than led by their inquiry and interest. Stealing moments of self-led discovery to insert a concept that we deem necessary for them to know (an approach of 'striking while the iron is hot' generated by pressure and fear) has led many a practitioner to close creative options down rather than open them up.

And just the fact that deviating from a lesson plan can require more work in terms of time, effort and lack of control over the outcomes can be off-putting. As Ward (2010) says, 'To some, it looks chaotic and unplanned' and the challenge 'for the adult world…is to hold back and resist the temptation to intervene and structure the child's encounter.' One of the essential tools that will aid us as we change is reflection. McNamee (2005, p.291) says of Paley, who can be considered a model in terms of creative and reflective practice, that 'she simply keeps reviewing and rethinking, comparing and wondering, and observing anew each day the experiences and behaviors of children in light of her own experiences – past and present.' Stott and Bowman (1996) believe that it is this kind of reflection that is central to cultivating excellence in teaching practice.

At this moment in time, we face an urgent decision: to continue to educate children traditionally with a focus on academic achievement at the expense of the arts, ascribing to our current, impoverished view of what literacy is and in the process continuing to risk the alienation of countless numbers of children or moving towards a more creative way of facilitating children's natural ways of learning and syncing our direction with their conation. Tim Lott (2017), writing in the *Guardian*, bemoans the lack of emphasis on and valuing of storytelling in schools, saying that:

> Storytelling is more than simply an art – it is a crucial skill for life and commerce. Politicians should know this better than anyone. What is 'Vote for us and the country will be strong and stable' if not a story? … Everything made of words is a story.

The UK government itself has expressed concern at this misplaced focus, with a recent parliamentary education committee stating, 'The Committee is concerned by the emphasis on technical aspects of writing and the diminished focus on composition and creativity at primary school' (UK Parliament 2017). The current culture of teaching to test, with an emphasis on technicality in primary schools, does not lead to gains in terms of literacy and may in fact rob children of the ability to begin to craft and tell imaginative stories. Confidence is built through episodes of competence, and as we focus more on grammar than on ideas we limit expression, and in turn the growth of confidence. As I was learning to write many years ago, we were – of course – taught how to structure sentences, and how to use punctuation correctly, how to identify and name parts of speech, and how to position apostrophes: the basics of good grammar. But we were never instructed to the point where it was off-putting in its complexity, causing me to lose interest in the expression of my ideas.

The answer to our questions about learning, about curriculum content and about pedagogy can all be answered with creativity. Creativity is essential and must be propagated from and in the earliest years, and it must follow children as they grow. We cannot allow them to be lost to the technicalities of literacy, forever shut off from the joy of uncovering knowledge and making it their own. The choice in terms of which way we proceed is ours. If we do, however, continue with the side lining of creativity in favour of what we view as more academic subjects, we risk 'that creativity will be crowded out by curricula that prioritize "know what" over "know how"' (Charman 2019).

Much work has, indeed, been done over the last few years in terms of developing more play-based curricula in the early years, and there has been an increased focus on the importance of creativity. We need to remain steadfast in these gains and continue to make them, as due to the rapid pace of societal and technological change, and a lack of enlightenment as to the skills and knowledge that will be needed for children 'to address the challenges they will face' (Duffy 2010, p.26), we cannot be sure about whether the content we teach them will be sufficient. But what we can be sure of is that 'a creative mind and a positive disposition towards others will be their best chance of addressing them' (ibid.).

If we consider children's intrinsic motivation to be central to our educating, understanding that it thrives on four key human needs: competence, autonomy, relatedness and purpose (Martela and Riekki 2018); if we look for and point to the human element in our learning content, understanding the mind's capacity and desire for narrative; if we focus on uncovering meaning; and if we marry this with the acquisition of skills in terms of decoding and composition and the grasping of concepts – we will be actively laying solid foundations for children in all aspects of learning. Foundations on which they can raise pillars of proficiency.

CONCLUSION

At a time when the world feels increasingly fragmented, experiencing what would appear to be an epidemic of loneliness caused by advances in technology and a decline in real connection, it would make sense to focus on facilitating the growth of excellent communicators who contribute to society as listeners, speakers, critical thinkers and evaluators of the information presented to them. What we are aiming for in all of our educating is for children to become creative citizens who prioritize connection with others and act in a compassionate manner – individuals who construct peaceful lives and, in turn, peaceful societies.

As humans, we possess an intrinsic longing for story. We are designed to tell our stories and to listen to those of others, seeking affirmation and commonality, and aiming to make sense of the world and, ultimately, to find meaning. As we share stories with children (the stories of their origins, their families, their societies and nations, humanity and the natural world, and of magical and mystical beings), as we engage them in fiction; and as they compose and tell their own stories – they begin to weave this knowledge together to forge both an inner voice and a personal narrative that is constantly growing and increasingly reflective.

The virtues and values contained within the stories we give to children – with just some being tenderness, kindness, compassion and fairness – can inspire, direct, heal and help them, beginning even to address any issues of loneliness, trauma and injustice they may have already experienced in their young lives. Children who cannot speak up for themselves may find, in story, a voice that sounds similar to their own, and the relief of that in itself can save them. This recognition, this identification, this finding of themselves in others can begin to build a sense of belonging that will sustain them throughout their childhood and beyond.

There is much that requires urgent attention in terms of children's education, health and happiness. Many children face a lifetime of struggle due to poverty, the long-term effects of adverse childhood experiences and inequality in terms of education, resulting in limited opportunities for success. There is, therefore, a crucial need to provide safe, nurturing early years experiences that help to improve health, learning outcomes and emotional well-being. And what stories do in meeting these needs is provide hope, a belief that things can be made better and sometimes a model for making them so. Joan Almon (n.d.) explains that:

> For young children fairy tales affirm that, yes, there are difficulties in life but we have the courage, strength, and steadfastness to meet them. And while our strength alone may not be enough, there are wonderful beings who come to our aid – kindly dwarves and animals, wise old men and women, and children themselves. The world of fairy tales is full of wonderful beings as well as evil ones. They strengthen the child's inner confidence that while terrible things sometimes happen, life is nevertheless good.

Can stories solve all of the world's problems? Certainly not. But what they can do is affect people deeply by accessing the parts of humanity that information and data cannot.

I believe that story is a powerful learning tool. At a time when there is constant debate over pedagogy and methodology, we continue to overlook our most ancient form of communication, one we are hardwired to engage in; and one which we do not need to teach but rather simply facilitate. As we invest in sourcing appropriate stories and begin to use methods of teaching that sync with children's need for embodied learning and socialization, I believe we will begin to see a return in terms of engagement and application. It is within our power to make learning relevant and meaningful to children: to make it matter.

And this approach does not need to be costly. Stories can be freely exchanged: told and sung, drawn and acted, composed alone or in collaboration with others. Even when in book form, they do not require ownership but can be accessed through libraries, schools, charities and clubs.

The author Michael Morpurgo advocates for half an hour of story time at the end of each day for all children in primary school, saying that children should go home reliving a story, wondering about it and dreaming about it (Morpurgo 2017). Why? Because it has the power to change them, and they will begin to see the world and others through a story lens: developing awareness, evaluating information, considering appearance versus reality, recognizing themes, hypothesizing alternative endings and creating them anew.

My wish for you is to embrace the power of storytelling for the children in your care. Encourage them to carefully listen as stories unfold, drinking in the magic of fiction and the knowledge of fact. Attend to them eagerly as they express themselves, looking and listening for their stories in all that they do, and responding with delight. Give them agency and autonomy: let them develop their own narratives, from the simple to the sensational. Allow story to bind you together as you find wonder in it, as it brings forth the deepest thought and the widest range of emotions. It is in our power as parents, practitioners and all those who work with children to begin to do this.

We cannot address every issue nor can we change every outcome, but what we can do is begin to use story to support healthy learning and development, to uncover meaning and purpose and to offer hope and healing both on an individual and a societal level.

Once upon a time…

Biographies

Helen Lumgair holds a BA (Hons) in early years teaching and a Montessori International Diploma, and is a Feuerstein Instrumental Enrichment Mediator. More recently, Helen designed and authored part of a narrative-based early years curriculum with an emphasis on developing empathy in the lives of young learners for the global non-governmental organization Think Equal, delivering training across numerous countries, with the programme now being implemented on a global scale.

Helen has authored a chapter on using the process of narrative to develop empathy in early childhood in the book *Developing Empathy in the Early Years: A Guide for Practitioners* and currently writes for the Novak Djokovic Foundation on early childhood development. She is an education advisor to the literary resource Tales Toolkit and is part of the oversight team of the Sure Starts Children's Centre in Tanzania.

Kanella Boukouvala is a person-centred counsellor and certified play therapist and supervisor. She is trained in play therapy, Theraplay®, filial play, emotional focused couples therapy (EFT), eye movement desensitization and reprocessing (EMDR), comprehensive resource model (CRM), dyadic developmental psychotherapy (DDP) and several other models that she uses in her work.

Nellie is a full member of Play Therapy International and the associate tutor for play therapy at Leeds Beckett University. She is the founder of Play Therapy Greece and works therapeutically with adults, children, adolescents, couples and families, as well as delivering play therapy training.

Helen Garnett co-founded a preschool in 2005, where she developed a keen interest in early intervention and the positive effect this has on a child's development and progress. In 2015 she became an early years consultant and author, working initially with Think Equal, a global initiative to promote empathy in young children, now being successfully implemented across five continents. Helen has written a book, *Developing Empathy in the Early Years: A Guide for Practitioners*, which won the Nursery World Awards Professional Book Category in 2018, and is currently writing a book for the Early Years Alliance on creating a resilient workforce in the early years. She writes articles for leading parent and early years organizations and publications such as Parenta and *Early Years Educator*.

Joanna Grace is a sensory engagement and inclusion specialist, author, trainer, TEDx speaker and founder of the Sensory Projects, which run on the principle that with the right knowledge and a little creativity, inexpensive sensory items can become effective tools for inclusion. The individual projects that make up the Sensory Projects have won awards and influenced practice nationally and internationally.

Dr Valerie Lovegreen has a doctorate of philosophy in psychology from Northcentral University, a Master's degree in communicative disorders from the University of Central Florida and a Bachelor of Arts degree in elementary education from Rhode Island College.

Currently, she works as a psychologist and a speech and language pathologist with clients aged from 2 years to adulthood in her private practice. Valerie specializes in cognitive and language therapy, assisting learners in developing thinking skills for academic and lifelong learning. She is a certified trainer in Feuerstein Instrumental Enrichment (Standard and Basic levels), and has training in Lindamood–Bell Learning Processes, Wilson Reading, Conscious Discipline, Balametrics, fast forword, Interactive Metronome and It Takes Two to Talk (Hanen Program).

Valerie has written extensively on critical thinking and narrative and her passion is interacting with children, teachers, therapists and parents to provide training, mentoring and therapy to improve thinking skills, communication and collaboration, and to enhance the quality of life of all with whom she works.

Dr Jo Van Herwegen, PhD, is an associate professor in the Department of Psychology and Human Development at UCL Institute of Education, London, and co-ordinator of the Child Development and Learning Difficulties Lab. Her research focuses mainly on language and number development in both typical and atypical populations, including Williams syndrome, autism spectrum disorders, Down syndrome and mathematical learning difficulties. She explores individual differences considering which cognitive abilities or strategies relate to successful performance, in order to aid the development of valid training programmes. Her research has been supported by various sources of research funding (e.g. British Academy, Nuffield Foundation and Baily Thomas Charitable Fund).

References

Adichie, C.N. (2009) 'The Danger of a Single Story.' TED Talk. Accessed on 19/8/2020 at www.ted.com/talks/chimamanda_ngozi_adichie_the_danger_of_a_single_story/transcript?language=en.

Agosto, D.E. (2016) 'Why storytelling matters: Unveiling the literacy benefits of storytelling.' Association for Library Service to Children 14, 2. Accessed on 20/8/2020 at https://journals.ala.org/index.php/cal/article/view/5990/7646.

Ahn, J. (2012) 'A review of the place of narrative in the early years: A way into literacy.' Educational Research 3, 8, 627–631.

Aizenman, N. (2018) What's the Difference between Children's Books in China and the US? San Francisco: KQED. Accessed on 6/7/2020 at www.kqed.org/mindshift/49961/whats-the-difference-between-childrens-books-in-china-and-the-u-s.

Albers, P. (2016) Why Stories Matter in Children's Learning. London: The Conversation Trust. Accessed on 6/7/2020 at https://theconversation.com/why-stories-matter-for-childrens-learning-52135.

Almon, J. (n.d.) 'Oral Language: The Foundation of Literacy.' Robertsbridge: Community Products. Accessed on 6/7/2020 at www.communityplaythings.co.uk/learning-library/articles/oral-language.

Applebee, A.N. (1977) 'A sense of story.' Theory into Practice 16, 5, 342–347.

Arizpe, E. (2013) 'Meaning-making from wordless (or nearly wordless) picturebooks: What educational research expects and what readers have to say.' Cambridge Journal of Education 43, 2, 163–176.

Arizpe, E., Colomer, T. and Martínez-Roldán, C. (2014) Visual Journeys through Wordless Narratives: An International Inquiry with Immigrant Children and the Arrival. London: Bloomsbury.

Ashiabi, G.S. (2007) 'Play in the preschool classroom: Its socioemotional significance and the teacher's role in play.' Early Childhood Education Journal 35, 199–207.

Balcomb, A. (2000) 'The Power of Narrative: Constituting Reality through Storytelling.' In P. Denis (ed.) Orality, Memory and the Past: Listening to the Voices of Black Clergy under Colonialism and Apartheid. Pietermaritzburg: Cluster Publications.

Bandura, A. (1997) Self-Efficacy: The Exercise of Control. New York: Freeman.

Bandura, A. (2002) 'Social Cognitive Theory of Mass Communication.' In J. Bryant and D. Zillmann (eds) Media Effects: Advances in Theory and Research (2nd ed.). Hillsdale, NJ: Erlbaum.

Barker, P. (1996) Psychotherapeutic Metaphors: A Guide to Theory and Practice. Bristol: Brunner/Mazel.

Barron, I. and Powell, J. (2002) 'Story Sacks, children's narratives and the social construction of reality.' Citizenship, Social and Economics Education 5, 3, 129–137.

Bateson, M.C. (2011) *Composing a Further Life*. London: Vintage Books.

Bay Area Early Childhood Funders (2007) *Play in the Early Years: Key to School Success*. El Cerrito: Bay Area Early Childhood Funders. Accessed on 6/7/2020 at www. researchconnections.org/childcare/resources/12471.

Beck, J. (2015) *Life's Stories*. Washington, DC: The Atlantic Monthly Group. Accessed on 6/7/2020 at www.theatlantic.com/health/archive/2015/08/life-stories-narrative-psychology-redemption-mental-health/400796.

Belet, S.D. and Dal, S. (2010) 'The use of storytelling to develop the primary school students' critical reading skill: The primary education pre-service teachers' opinions.' *Procedia – Social and Behavioral Sciences 9*, 1830–1834.

Bellace, M. (2011) 'How to get high naturally.' Workshop at Lynn University, Florida, 17 October.

Berliner, W. (2020) 'Schools Are Killing Curiosity': Why We Need to Stop Telling Children to Shut Up and Learn. New York: Guardian News & Media. Accessed on 6/7/2020 at www.theguardian.com/education/2020/jan/28/schools-killing-curiosity-learn.

Bigozzi, L. and Vettori, G. (2016) 'To tell a story, to write it: Developmental patterns of narrative skills from preschool to first grade.' *European Journal of Psychology of Education 31*, 4, 461–477.

Bliss, L.S. and McCabe, A. (2008) 'Patterns of discourse coherence: Variations in genre performance in children with language impairment.' *Imagination, Cognition and Personality 28*, 2, 137–154.

Bliss, L.S. and McCabe, A. (2012) 'Personal narratives: Assessment and intervention.' *Perspectives on Language Learning and Education 19*, 4, 117–154.

Bliss, L.S., McCabe, A. and Miranda, A.E. (1998) 'Narrative assessment profile: Discourse analysis for school-age children.' *Journal of Communication Disorders 31*, 4, 347–363.

Blom, E. and Boerma, T. (2016) 'Why do children with language impairment have difficulties with narrative macrostructure?' *Research in Developmental Disabilities 55*, 301–311.

BookTrust (2020) *Representation of people of colour among children's book creators in the UK*. London: BookTrust Represents. Accessed on 10/12/2020 at https://www.booktrust.org.uk/news-and-features/news/news-2020/representation-in-childrens-books-still-not-reflective-of-society-says-booktrust-and-clpe.

Borba, M. (2016) *UnSelfie: Why Empathetic Kids Succeed in Our All-About-Me World*. New York: Touchstone Books.

Brady, J. (2018) *Survey: State School Teachers Say Much of Their Work Is Meaningless*. London: The Conversation Trust. Accessed on 6/7/2020 at https://theconversation.com/survey-state-school-teachers-say-much-of-their-work-is-meaningless-95803.

Bransford, J.D. and Stein, B.S. (1993) *The Ideal Problem Solver*. New York: W.H. Freeman.

Brennan, C. (2008) *Partners in Play: How Children Organise their Participation in Sociodramatic Play*. Doctoral Thesis, Technological University Dublin. Accessed on 18/01/2021 at https://arrow.tudublin.ie/cgi/viewcontent.cgi?article=1010&context=appadoc.

Britton, J. (1970) *Language and Learning*. Coral Gables, FL: University of Miami Press.

Brod, G., Hasselhorn, M. and Bunge, S.A. (2018) 'When generating a prediction boosts learning: The element of surprise.' *Learning and Instruction 55*, 22–31.

Brown, B. (2013) *Daring Greatly: How the Courage to Be Vulnerable Transforms the Way We Live, Love, Parent, and Lead*. London: Penguin.

Brown, B. (2015) *Rising Strong*. London: Vermilion.

Brown, B. (2018) *Courage and Power from Pain: An Interview with Viola Davis.* Houston: Brené Brown. Accessed on 6/7/2020 at https://brenebrown.com/blog/2018/05/09/courage-power-pain-interview-viola-davis.

Bruner, J. (1986) *Actual Minds, Possible Worlds.* Cambridge, MA: Harvard University Press.

Bruner, J. (1990) *Acts of Meaning.* Cambridge, MA: Harvard University Press.

Buechner, F. (2019) *Your Own Journey.* Cambridge: Frederich Buechner Center. Accessed on 6/7/2020 at www.frederickbuechner.com/quote-of-the-day/2019/1/11/your-own-journey?rq=the%20story%20of%20any%20one%20of%20us.

Burke, A. (2012) 'Empowering children's voices through the narrative of drawings.' *The Morning Watch Education and Social Analysis 40*, 1–2, 1–14.

Burke, L.A. (2007) *Developing Young Thinkers: Discovering Baseline Understandings of Effective Thinking among Children and Teachers and Intervening to Enhance Thinking Skills.* Doctoral thesis, University of Edinburgh. Accessed on 6/7/2020 at https://pdfs.semanticscholar.org/281b/236d29016ae45d0c5254a45b410ca361fec2.pdf.

Burnard, P., Craft, A. and Grainger, T. (2006) 'Possibility thinking.' *International Journal of Early Years Education 14*, 3, 243–262.

Burns, G.W. (2005) *101 Healing Stories for Kids and Teens: Using Metaphors in Therapy.* Hoboken: Wiley.

Burns, M. (2019) *I'm a Neuroscientist. Here's How Teachers Change Kids' Brains.* Portland: EdSurge. Accessed on 6/7/2020 at www.edsurge.com/news/2019-02-19-i-m-a-neuroscientist-here-s-how-teachers-change-kids-brains.

Byrne, C.C. (ed.) (2010) *All That Was Lost – Apartheid Violence: Thirty TRC Participants Speak.* Benoni: Shereno Printers.

Cameron, L. and Rutland, A. (2006) 'Extended contact through story reading in school: Reducing children's prejudice toward the disabled.' *Journal of Social Issues 62*, 469–488.

Cameron, L., Rutland, A., Brown, R. and Douch, R. (2006) 'Changing children's intergroup attitudes toward refugees: Testing different models of extended contact.' *Child Development 77*, 1208–1219.

Cameron, L., Rutland, A., Hossain, R. and Petley, R. (2011) 'When and why does extended contact work? The role of high quality direct contact and group norms in the development of positive ethnic intergroup attitudes amongst children.' *Group Processes and Intergroup Relations 14*, 193–206.

Carlson, R. (2001) 'Therapeutic use of story in therapy with children.' *Guidance & Counseling 16*, 3, 92–99.

Carrazza, C. and Levine, S.C. (2019) 'How numbers are presented in counting books matters for children's learning: A parent-delivered intervention.' In *2019 SRCD Biennial Meeting.* Baltimore: Society for Research in Child Development.

Cartledge, G. and Kiarie, M. (2001) 'Learning social skills through literature for children and adolescents.' *Teaching Exceptional Children 34*, 2, 40–47.

Cattanach, A. (2008) *Play Therapy with Abused Children.* London: Jessica Kingsley Publishers.

Centre for Literacy in Primary Education (2018) *Reflecting Realities: Survey of Ethnic Diversity in UK Children's Books.* London: CLPE. Accessed on 19/8/2020 at https://clpe.org.uk/library-and-resources/research/reflecting-realities-survey-ethnic-representation-within-uk-children.

Centre for Literacy in Primary Education (2020) *Reflecting Realitites: Survey of Ethnic Representation within UK Children's Literature 2019*. London: CLPE. Accessed on 10/12/2020 at https://clpe.org.uk/clpes-reflecting-realities-survey-ethnic-representation-within-uk-children%E2%80%99s-literature-published.

Charman, H. (2019) 'Why Is It Important to Develop Learners' Creativity in the 21st Century?' In R. Gawn (ed.) *Creating Creators: How Can We Enhance Creativity in Education Systems?* Billund: Lego Foundation. Accessed on 6/7/2020 at www.legofoundation.com/media/1664/creating-creators_full-report.pdf.

Cheung, C.S., Monroy, J.A. and Delany, D.E. (2017) 'Learning-related values in young children's storybooks: An investigation in the United States, China, and Mexico.' *Journal of Cross-Cultural Psychology 48*, 4, 532–541.

Chouinard, M.M., Harris, P.L. and Maratsos, M.P. (2007) 'Children's Questions: A Mechanism for Cognitive Development.' *Monographs of the Society for Research in Child Development 72*, 1, i–129.

Cobley, P. (2001) *Narrative*. London: Routledge.

Cojocariu, V. and Butnaru, C. (2014) 'Asking questions – Critical thinking tools.' *Procedia – Social and Behavioral Sciences 128*, 22–28.

Colomer, T., Kümmerling-Meibauer, B. and Silva-Díaz, C. (eds) (2010) *New Directions in Picturebook Research*. New York: Taylor & Francis.

Colorado State University (2011) *Reading. Writing@CSU, Colorado State University*. [Online]. Accessed on 6/7/2020 at http://writing.colostate.edu/guides/guide.cfm?guideid=31 .

Community Products (2012a) *Block Play and Literacy*. Robertsbridge: Community Products. Accessed on 6/7/2020 at www.communityplaythings.co.uk/learning-library/blog/2012/january/block-play-and-literacy.

Community Products (2012b) *Story-Telling with Blocks*. Robertsbridge: Community Products. Accessed on 6/7/2020 at www.communityplaythings.co.uk/learning-library/blog/2012/june/story-telling-with-blocks.

Cox Gurdon, M. (2019) *The Enchanted Hour: The Miraculous Power of Reading Aloud in the Age of Distraction*. London: Piatkus.

Craft, A. (2000) *Creativity across the Primary Curriculum*. London: Routledge.

Craft, A. (2001) 'Little c Creativity.' In A. Craft, B. Jeffrey and M. Leibling (eds) *Creativity in Education*. London: Continuum.

Craft, A. (2002) *Creativity and Early Years Education*. London: Continuum.

Craft, A. (n.d.) *Creativity and Possibility in the Early Years*. Northamptonshire: TACTYC. Accessed on 6/7/2020 at https://tactyc.org.uk/pdfs/Reflection-craft.pdf.

Crawford, P. and Hade, D. (2000) 'Inside the picture, outside the frame: Semiotics and the reading of wordless picture books.' *Journal of Research in Childhood Education 15*, 1, 66–80.

Cremin, T., Burnard, P. and Craft, A. (2006) 'Pedagogy and possibility thinking in the early years.' *Thinking Skills and Creativity 1*, 2, 108–119.

Cremin, T., Chappell, K. and Craft, A. (2013) 'Reciprocity between narrative, questioning and imagination in the early and primary years: Examining the role of narrative in possibility thinking.' *Thinking Skills and Creativity 9*, 135–151.

Crossley, M.L. (2000) *Introducing Narrative Psychology: Self, Trauma and the Construction of Meaning*. Milton Keynes: Open University Press.

David, L. (2020) *Multiliteracies (New London Group)*. New York: Learning Theories. Accessed on 6/7/2020 at www.learning-theories.com/multiliteracies-new-london-group.html.

Day, L., Hanson, K., Maltby, J., Proctor, C. and Wood, A. (2010) 'Hope uniquely predicts objective academic achievement above intelligence, personality, and previous academic achievement.' *Journal of Research in Personality 44*, 550–553.

de la Peña, M. (2018) 'Why We Shouldn't Shield Children from Darkness.' Sacramento: Time USA. Accessed on 6/7/2020 at https://time.com/5093669/why-we-shouldnt-shield-children-from-darkness.

Department of Basic Education (2015) 'National Book Week.' Accessed on 19/8/2020 at www.education.gov.za/Newsroom/OpinionPieces/tabid/609/ctl/Details/mid/1909/ItemID/3137 /Default.aspx.

Dickinson, D.K., Griffith, J.A., Michnick Golinkoff, R. and Hirsh-Pasek, K. (2012) 'How reading books fosters language development around the world.' *Child Development Research*, art. 602807.

Doucleff, M. and Greenhalgh, J. (2019) 'How Inuit Parents Teach Kids to Control Their Anger.' San Francisco: KQED. Accessed on 6/7/2020 at www.kqed.org/mindshift/53283/how-inuit-parents-teach-kids-to-control-their-anger.

Dowhower, S. (1997) 'Wordless books: Promise and possibilities, a genre come of age.' *Yearbook of the American Reading Forum 17*, 57–79.

Duffy, B. (2010) 'Using Creativity and Creative Learning to Enrich the Lives of Young Children at the Thomas Coram Centre.' In C. Tims (ed.) *Born Creative*. London: Demos. Accessed on 6/7/2020 at https://dera.ioe.ac.uk/23207/1/Born_Creative_-_web_-_final.pdf.

Dunn, M. (2001) 'Aboriginal literacy: Reading the tracks.' *The Reading Teacher 54*, 7, 678–687.

Egan, K. (1986) *Teaching as Story Telling: An Alternative Approach to Teaching and Curriculum in the Elementary School*. London: University of Western Ontario.

Ellyatt, W. (2010) 'A Science of Learning: New Approaches to Thinking About Creativity in the Early Years.' In C. Tims (ed.) *Born Creative*. London: Demos. Accessed on 6/7/2020 at https://dera.ioe.ac.uk/23207/1/Born_Creative_-_web_-_final.pdf.

Elvin, L. (1977) *The Place of Common Sense in Educational Thought*. London: Unwin Educational.

Engel, S. (1996) 'The guy who went up the steep nicken: The emergence of story telling during the first three years.' *Zero to Three 17*, 3, 1–9.

Engel, S. (2011) 'Children's need to know: Curiosity in schools.' *Harvard Educational Review 81*, 4, 625–645.

Engel, S. (2016) *Storytelling in the First Three Years*. Washington, DC: Zero to three. Accessed on 6/7/2020 at www.zerotothree.org/resources/1057-storytelling-in-the-first-three-years.

Erikson, M.H., Rossi, E.L. and Rossi, S.I. (1976) *Hypnotic Realities*. New York: Irvington Publishers.

Esfahani Smith, S.E. (2017) *The Power of Meaning: The True Route to Happiness*. London: Penguin Random House.

Fassler, J. (2011) *Maurice Sendak's Long History of Scaring Kids (and Their Parents)*. Washington, DC: The Atlantic Monthly Group. Accessed on 6/7/2020 at www.theatlantic.com/entertainment/archive/2011/09/maurice-sendaks-long-history-of-scaring-kids-and-their-parents/245339.

Fassler, J. (2012) *Maurice Sendak Scared Children Because He Loved Them*. Washington, DC: The Atlantic Monthly Group. Accessed on 6/7/2020 at www.theatlantic.com/entertainment/archive/2012/05/maurice-sendak-scared-children-because-he-loved-them/256928.

Ferguson, D. (2018) *Must Monsters Always Be Male? Huge Gender Bias Revealed in Children's Books*. New York: Guardian News & Media. Accessed on 6/7/2020 at www.theguardian.com/books/2018/jan/21/childrens-books-sexism-monster-in-your-kids-book-is-male.

Feuerstein, R. and Lewin-Benham, A. (2012) *What Learning Looks Like: Mediated Learning in Theory and Practice*. New York: Teachers College Press.

Flood, A. (2018) *'Mum This Is Me!': The Pop-Up Bookshop That Only Sells Diverse Children's Books*. New York: Guardian News & Media. Accessed on 6/7/2020 at www.theguardian.com/books/2018/dec/14/readtheonepercent-brixton-bookshop-knights-of.

Flood, A. (2020) *Children's books eight times as likely to feature animal main characters as BAME people*. New York: Guardian News & Media. Accessed on 10/12/2020 at https://www.theguardian.com/books/2020/nov/11/childrens-books-eight-times-as-likely-to-feature-animal-main-characters-than-bame-people.

Fountain, S. (1999) *Peace Education in UNICEF*. Working Paper, Education Section, Programme Division. New York: UNICEF.

Fox Eades, J.M. (2006) *Classroom Tales: Using Storytelling to Build Emotional, Social and Academic Skills across the Primary Curriculum*. London: Jessica Kingsley Publishers.

Friday, M.J. (2014) 'Why Storytelling in the Classroom Matters.' San Rafael: George Lucas Educational Foundation. Accessed on 6/7/2020 at www.edutopia.org/blog/storytelling-in-the-classroom-matters-matthew-friday.

Garnett, H. (2017) *Developing Empathy in the Early Years: A Guide for Practitioners*. London: Jessica Kingsley Publishers.

Gay, G. (2013) 'Teaching to and through cultural diversity.' *Curriculum Inquiry 43*, 1, 48–70.

Göbel, S.M., McCrink, K., Fischer, M.H. and Shaki, S. (2018) 'Observation of directional storybook reading influences young children's counting direction.' *Journal of Experimental Child Psychology 166*, 49–66.

Goleman, D. (2006) *Social Intelligence: The New Science of Human Relationships*. New York: Bantam Dell.

Gopnik, A.M., Meltzoff, A.N. and Kuhl, P.K. (2007) *The Scientist in the Crib: What Early Learning Tells Us About the Mind*. New York: Harper Collins.

Gottschall, J. (2013) *The Storytelling Animal: How Stories Make Us Human*. Boston: First Mariner Books.

Grace, J. (2014) *Sensory Stories for Children and Teens with Special Educational Needs: A Practical Guide*. London: Jessica Kingsley Publishers.

Gray, P. (2014) *One More Really Big Reason to Read Stories to Children*. New York: Sussex Publishers. Accessed on 6/7/2020 at www.psychologytoday.com/intl/blog/freedom-learn/201410/one-more-really-big-reason-read-stories-children.

Griffiths, A. (2011) *The Naked Boy and the Crocodile: Stories by Children from Remote Indigenous Communities*. Sydney: Macmillan.

Groff, P. (1974) 'Children's Literature Versus Wordless "Books".' *Top of the News 30*, 294–303.

Hamber, B., Nageng, D. and O'Malley, G. (2000) '"Telling it like it is…": Understanding the Truth and Reconciliation Commission from the perspective of survivors.' *Psychology in Society 26*, 18–42.

Hare, J. (2011) '"They tell a story and there's meaning behind that story": Indigenous knowledge and young Indigenous children's literacy learning.' *Journal of Early Childhood Literacy 12*, 4, 389–414.

Haven, K. (2007) *Story Proof: The Science Behind the Startling Power of Story*. Exeter: Libraries Unlimited.

Hearn, B. (1992) 'The mythical child: Patterns of sound, sight and story.' Paper presented at Erikson Institute, Chicago, IL.

Hobson, T. (2019) 'Yes, I'm Savoring It.' Seattle: Thomas Hobson. Accessed on 6/7/2020 at http://teachertomsblog.blogspot.com/2019/01/yes-im-savoring-.

Hobson, T. (2020) *The Having of Wonderful Ideas*. Seattle: Thomas Hobson. Accessed on 6/7/2020 at http://teachertomsblog.blogspot.com/2020/05/the-having-of-wonderful-ideas.html?utm_source=feedburner&utm_medium=email&utm_campaign=Feed%3A+TeacherTom+%28Teacher+Tom%29.

Holland, N.N. (1975) *5 Readers Reading*. New Haven: Yale University Press.

Hong, L.T. (1993) *Two of Everything*. Park Ridge: Albert Whitman.

Hornberger, N.H. (2009) 'Multilingual education policy and practice: Ten certainties (grounded in Indigenous experience).' *Language Teaching 42*, 1, 197–211.

Horner, L., Kadiwal, L., Sayed, Y., Barrett, A., Durrani, N. and Novelli, M. (2015) *Literature Review: The Role of Teachers in Peacebuilding*. Amsterdam: Research Consortium on Education and Peacebuilding, UNICEF & Learning for Peace.

Hough, L. (2017) *But That's A Girl Book!* Cambridge: Harvard Graduate School of Education. Accessed on 6/7/2020 at www.gse.harvard.edu/news/ed/17/08/girl-book.

Huitt, W. and Cain, S. (2005) *An Overview of the Conative Domain*. Valdosta: Valdosta State University. Accessed on 6/7/2020 at http://citeseerx.ist.psu.edu/viewdoc/download? doi=10.1.1.363.9158&rep=rep1&type=pdf.

Hull, G.A., Mikulecky, L., St. Clair, R. and Kerka, S. (2003) *Multiple Literacies: A Compilation for Adult Educators*. Ohio: Center in Education Training for Employment.

Hutton, J.S., Phelan, K., Horowitz-Kraus, T., Dudley, J. *et al.* (2017) 'Shared reading quality and brain activation during story listening in preschool-age children.' *Journal of Pediatrics 191*, 204–211.

Hutton, J.S., Huang, G., Sahay, R., Dewitt, T. and Ittenbach, R. (2020) 'A novel, composite measure of screen-based media use in young children (ScreenQ) and associations with parenting practices and cognitive abilities.' *Pediatric Research 87*, 1211–1218.

IMDB (n.d.) *Cry Freedom*. Seattle: IMDB. Accessed on 6/7/2020 at www.imdb.com/title/tt0092804.

Iseke, J. (2013) 'Indigenous storytelling as research.' *International Review of Qualitative Research 6*, 4, 559–577.

Istance, D. and Paniagua, A. (2019) *Learning to Leapfrog: Innovative Pedagogies to Transform Education*. Washington, DC: Center for Universal Education at Brookings. Accessed on 6/7/2020 at www.brookings.edu/wp-content/uploads/2019/09/Learning-to-Leapfrog-Policy-Brief-Web.pdf.

Iturbe, A. (2019) *The Librarian of Auschwitz*. London: Ebury Press.

Jalongo, M.R., Dragich, D., Conrad, N.K. and Zhang, A. (2002) 'Using wordless picture books to support emergent literacy.' *Early Childhood Education Journal 29*, 3, 167–177.

Jeffrey, B. (2001) 'Primary pupils' perspectives and creative learning.' *Encyclopedia 9*, 133–152 (Italian journal).

Jeffrey, B. and Craft, A. (2004) 'Teaching creatively and teaching for creativity: Distinctions and relationships.' *Educational Studies 30*, 1, 77–87.

Jenkins, J.M. and Astington, J.W. (2000) 'Theory of mind and social behavior: Casual models tested in a longitudinal study.' *Merrill-Palmer Quarterly 46*, 203–220.

Jent, J.F., Niec, L.N. and Baker, S.E. (2011) 'Play and Interpersonal Processes.' In S.W. Russ and L.N. Niec (eds) *Play in Clinical Practice: Evidence-Based Approaches*. New York: Guilford Press.

Johnson, M. (1987) *The Body in the Mind: The Bodily Basis of Meaning, Imagination, and Reason.* Chicago: University of Chicago Press.

Johnson, S. (2009) 'This little chicken went to Africa.' Unpublished MPhil thesis in Visual Arts, Stellenbosch University.

Kamenetz, A. (2018) *What's Going On in Your Child's Brain When You Read Them a Story?* San Francisco: KQED. Accessed on 6/7/2020 at www.kqed.org/mindshift/51281/whats-going-on-in-your-childs-brain-when-you-read-them-a-story.

Kaplan, E. (2020) *Mo Willems on the Lost Art of Being Silly.* San Rafael: George Lucas Educational Foundation. Accessed on 6/7/2020 at www.edutopia.org/article/mo-willems-lost-art-being-silly.

Kaufman, S.B. (2011) *The Will and Ways of Hope.* New York: Sussex Publishers. Accessed on 6/7/2020 at www.psychologytoday.com/us/blog/beautiful-minds/201112/the-will-and-ways-hope.

Kaufman, S.B. (2012) *The Need for Pretend Play in Child Development.* New York: Sussex Publishers. Accessed on 6/7/2020 at www.psychologytoday.com/us/blog/beautiful-minds/201203/the-need-pretend-play-in-child-development.

Kemp, C. (2015) 'MRI shows association between reading to young children and brain activity.' *American Academy of Pediatrics News 36*, 10. Accessed 6/7/2020 at www.aappublications.org/content/early/2015/04/25/aapnews.20150425-4.

Kerby, A.P. (1991) *Narrative and the Self.* Indiana: Indiana State Press.

Khan, K.S., Gugiu, M.R., Justice, L.M., Bowles, R.P., Skibbe, L.E. and Piasta, S.B. (2016) 'Age-related progressions in story structure in young children's narratives.' *Journal of Speech, Language, and Hearing Research 59*, 6, 1395–1408.

Kinnear, V. and Clark, J. (2014) 'Probabilistic Reasoning and Prediction with Young Children.' In J. Anderson, M. Cavanaugh and A. Prescott (eds) *Curriculum in Focus: Research Guided Practice. Proceedings of the 37th Annual Conference of the Mathematics Education Research Group of Australasia.* Sydney: Mathematics Education Research Group of Australasia.

Klass, P. (2017) *Literacy Builds Life Skills as Well as Language Skills.* New York: New York Times. Accessed on 6/7/2020 at www.nytimes.com/2017/10/16/well/family/literacy-builds-life-skills-as-well-as-language-skills.html.

Kolb, K. (1990) 'Humor is no laughing matter.' *Early Report 18*, 1. University of Minnesota, Center for Early Education and Development.

Labov, W. (2006) 'Narrative pre-construction.' *Narrative Inquiry 16*, 1, 37–45.

le Roux, A. (2012) 'The Production and Use of Wordless Picturebooks in Parent-Child Reading: An Exploratory Study Within a South African Context.' Unpublished MPhil thesis in Visual Arts (stream illustration): Stellenbosch University.

le Roux, A. (2017) 'An Exploration of the Potential of Wordless Picturebooks to Encourage Parent–Child Reading in the South African Context.' Doctoral thesis, Stellenbosch University. Accessed on 6/7/2020 at https://scholar.sun.ac.za/handle/10019.1/100920.

Leslie, A.M. (1987) 'Pretense and representation: The origins of "theory of mind."' *Psychological Review 94*, 412–426.

Lessing, D. (2007) *On Not Winning the Nobel Prize.* Stockholm: Nobel Media AB. Accessed on 6/7/2020 at www.nobelprize.org/prizes/literature/2007/lessing/25434-doris-lessing-nobel-lecture-2007.

Levy, E.T. and McNeill, D. (2015) *Narrative Development in Young Children: Gesture, Imagery, and Cohesion.* Cambridge: Cambridge University Press.

Little, J. (2001) *Orphan at My Door: The Home Child Diary of Victoria Cope.* Markham, ON: Scholastic.

Liu, C.C., Liu, K.P., Chen, G.D. and Liu, B.J. (2010) 'Children's collaborative storytelling with linear and nonlinear approaches.' *Procedia – Social and Behavioral Sciences 2,* 2, 4787–4792.

Lott, T. (2017) *Ditch the Grammar and Teach Children Storytelling Instead.* New York: Guardian News & Media. Accessed on 6/7/2020 at www.theguardian.com/lifeandstyle/2017/may/19/ditch-the-grammar-and-teach-children-storytelling-instead.

Louw, D.A. and Louw A.E. (2014) *Child and Adolescent Development* (2nd ed.). Bloemfontein: Psychology Publications.

Lovegreen, V. and Lumgair, H. (2016) *Think Equal Early Years Curriculum Framework.* Accessed on 22/08/2017 at www.thinkequal.com/whoweare.

Low, G., Todd, Z., Deigan, A. and Cameron, L. (eds) (2010) *Researching and Applying Metaphor in the Real World.* Amsterdam: John Benjamins.

Machado, J. (2010) *Early Childhood Experiences in Language Arts: Early Literacy.* Belmont, CA: Wadsworth Cengage Learning.

MacIntyre, A. (1981) *After Virtue.* Notre Dame, IN: University of Notre Dame Press.

Maher, M. and Bellen, L. (2015) 'Smoothing children's transition into formal schooling: Addressing complexities in an early literacy initiative in remote Aboriginal communities, Northern Territory, Australia.' *Early Childhood Education Journal 43,* 1, 9–17.

Maich, K. and Kean, S. (2004) 'Read two books and write me in the morning! Bibliotherapy for social emotional intervention in the inclusive classroom.' *Teaching Exceptional Children Plus 1,* 2, art. 5.

Mäkinen, L., Loukusa, S., Nieminen, L., Leinonen, E. and Kunnari, S. (2014) 'The development of narrative productivity, syntactic complexity, referential cohesion and event content in four- to eight-year-old Finnish children.' *First Language 34,* 1, 24–42.

Martela, M. and Riekki, J.J. (2018) 'Autonomy, competence, relatedness, and beneficence: A multicultural comparison of the four pathways to meaningful work.' *Frontiers in Psychology 9,* art. 1157.

McAdams, D.P. and McLean, K.C. (2013) 'Narrative identity.' *Current Directions in Psychological Science 22,* 3, 233–238.

McAdams, D.P. and Manczak, E. (2015) 'Personality and the Life Story.' In M. Mikulincer and P.R. Shaver (eds) *APA Handbook of Personality and Social Psychology.* Washington, DC: American Psychological Association.

McCombs, B.L. (1996) 'Alternative Perspectives for Motivation.' In L. Baker, P. Afflerbach and D. Reinking (eds) *Developing Engaged Readers in School and Home Communities.* Mahwah, NJ: Erlbaum.

McConnell, G.E. (2011) *Story Presentation Effects on the Narratives of Preschool Children from Low and Middle Socioeconomic Homes.* Doctoral thesis, University of Kansas. Accessed on 6/7/2020 at https://kuscholarworks.ku.edu/handle/1808/8169.

McKeough, A., Bird, S., Tourigny, E., Romaine, A. *et al.* (2008) 'Storytelling as a foundation to literacy development for aboriginal children: Culturally and developmentally appropriate practices.' *Canadian Psychology 49,* 2, 148–154.

McLean, K.C., Pasupathi, M. and Pals, J.L. (2007) 'Selves creating stories creating selves: A process model of self-development.' *Personality and Social Psychology Review 11,* 3, 262–278.

McNamee, G.D. (2005) '"The one who gathers children": The work of Vivian Gussin Paley and current debates about how we educate young children.' *Journal of Early Childhood Teacher Education 25,* 3, 275–296.

McTavish, A. (2006) *Helping Children Manage Their Feelings*. Robertsbridge: Community Products. Accessed on 6/7/2020 at www.communityplaythings.co.uk/learning-library/articles/helping-children-manage-their-feelings.

Merriam-Webster (2019) *Empathy*. Springfield: Merriam-Webster. Accessed on 6/7/2020 at www.merriam-webster.com/dictionary/empathy.

Me Too movement (n.d.) *History & Vision*. New York: Me Too Movement. Accessed on 6/7/2020 at https://metoomvmt.org/about/.

Michnick Golinkoff, R. and Hirsh-Pasek, K. (2016) *Becoming Brilliant: What Science Tells Us about Raising Successful Children*. Washington, DC: American Psychological Association.

Miller, P.J., Chen, E.C. and Olivarez, M. (2014) 'Narrative making and remaking in the early years: Prelude to the personal narrative.' *New Directions for Child and Adolescent Development*, 145, 15–27.

Miller, P., Mintz, J., Hoogstra, L., Fung, H. and Potts, R. (1992) The narrated self: Young children's construction of self in relation to others in conversational stories of personal experience. *Merrill-Palmer Quarterly 38*, 1, 45–67.

Mills, J.C. and Crowley, R.J. (1986) *Therapeutic Metaphors for Children and the Child Within*. New York: Routledge.

Mills, J.C. and Crowley, R.J. (2014) *Therapeutic Metaphors for Children and the Child Within* (2nd ed). New York: Routledge.

Mix, K.S., Sandhofer, C.M., Moore, J.A. and Russell, C. (2012) 'Acquisition of the cardinal word principle: The role of input.' *Early Childhood Research Quarterly 27*, 2, 274–283.

Mokhtar, N.H., Halim, M.F.A. and Kamarulzaman, S.Z.S. (2011) 'The effectiveness of storytelling in enhancing communicative skills.' *Procedia – Social and Behavioral Sciences 18*, 163–169.

Moll, L.C., Amanti, C., Neff, D. and Gonzalez, N. (1992) 'Funds of knowledge for teaching: Using a qualitative approach to connect homes and classrooms.' Accessed on 18/8/2020 at https://education.ucsc.edu/ellisa/pdfs/Moll_Amanti_1992_Funds_of_Knowledge.pdf.

Mooney, B. (2018) *The Greatest Gift for a Child This Christmas? Read Them a Story! Bel Mooney on the Ultimate Way to Boost Your Kids' Concentration and Leave Them with a Lifetime of Memories*. London: Associated Newspapers. Accessed on 7/7/2020 at www.dailymail.co.uk/femail/article-6448659/The-greatest-gift-child-Christmas-Read-story-says-BEL-MOONEY.html?ito=email_share_article-drawer.

Mooney, C.G. (2005) *Use Your Words: How Teacher Talk Helps Children Learn*. Corona: Redleaf Press.

Moreau, M.R. (2010) *The Importance of Narrative Development in School and in Life*. Springfield: MindWing Concepts. Accessed on 7/7/2020 at https://mindwingconcepts.com/blogs/news/36164033-the-importance-of-narrative-development-in-school-and-in-life.

Morpurgo, M. (2017) *The Power of Stories: Michael Morpurgo's Full Book Trust Lecture*. London: The Royal Society of Literature. Accessed on 7/7/2020 at https://rsliterature.org/lm-hub-post/the-power-of-stories-michael-morpurgos-full-book-trust-lecture.

Morris, H. (2007) 'Tall enough? An illustrator's visual enquiry into the production and consumption of isiXhosa picture books in South Africa.' Unpublished master's thesis, University of Stellenbosch.

The Moth (n.d.) *The Story Behind the Stories*. New York: The Moth. Accessed on 7/7/2020 at https://themoth.org/about.

Neuman, S.B. (2006) 'The Knowledge Gap: Implications for Early Education.' In S.B. Neuman and D.K. Dickinson (eds) *Handbook of Early Literacy Research* (vol. 2). New York: Guilford Press.

New York Times (1988) '*Cry Freedom* Seized by South African Police.' 30 July, p.6.

Nicolopoulou, A. (2007) 'The Interplay of Play and Narrative in Children's Development: Theoretical Reflections and Concrete Examples in Play and Development.' In A. Goncu and S. Gaskins (eds) *Evolutionary, Sociocultural, and Functional Perspectives.* Hove: Erlbaum.

Nicolopoulou, A., Cortina, K.S., Ilgaz, H., Cates, C.B. and de Sá, A.B. (2015) 'Using a narrative- and play-based activity to promote low-income preschoolers' oral language, emergent literacy, and social competence.' *Early Childhood Research Quarterly 31*, 147–162.

Nicolopoulou, A., McDowell, J. and Brockmeyer, C. (2006) 'Narrative play and emergent literacy: Storytelling and story-acting.' In D.G. Singer, R.M. Golinkoff and K. Hirsh-Pasek (eds) *Play = Learning: How Play Motivates and Enhances Children's Cognitive and Social-Emotional Growth.* New York: Oxford University Press.

Nikolajeva, M. and Scott, C. (2001) *How Picturebooks Work.* New York: Garland Publishing.

Noddings, N. (n.d.) 'The Use of Stories in Teaching.' Accessed on 7/7/2020 at http://personal.cege.umn.edu/~smith/docs/Noddings-The_use_of_stories_in_teaching-NPCT-1997-Ch2.pdf.

Nodelman, P. (1988) *Words about Pictures: The Narrative Art of Children's Picture Books.* Georgia: University of Georgia Press.

Norton, D.E. (1983) *Through the Eyes of a Child: an Introduction to Children's Literature.* Ohio: Charles E. Merrill Publishing.

Ntuli, C.D. (2011) 'From oral performance to picture books: A perspective on Zulu children's literature.' Unpublished PhD thesis, University of South Africa.

O'Carroll, S. and Hickman, R. (2012) *Narrowing the Literacy Gap: Strengthening Language and Literacy Development Between Birth and Six Years for Children in South Africa.* Cape Town: Wordworks.

Olsson, L.M. (2013) 'Taking children's questions seriously: The need for creative thought.' *Global Studies of Childhood 3*, 3, 230–253.

O'Neill, D.K., Pearce, M.J. and Pick, J.L. (2004) 'Preschool children's narratives and performance on the Peabody Individual Achievement Test-Revised: Evidence of a relation between early narrative and later mathematical ability.' *First Language 24*, 2, 149–183.

Oppenheim, D. and Warren, A.N.S. (1997) 'Emotion regulation in mother–child narrative co-construction: Associations with children's narratives and adaptation.' *Developmental Psychology 33*, 2, 284–294.

Pack, J. (2016) 'Learning stories.' *Teaching Young Children 9*, 2. Accessed on 7/7/2020 at www.naeyc.org/resources/pubs/tyc/dec2016/learning-stories.

Paley, V.G. (1988) *Bad Guys Don't Have Birthdays: Fantasy Play at Four.* Chicago: University of Chicago Press.

Paley, V.G. (1990) *The Boy Who Would Be a Helicopter.* Cambridge, MA: Harvard University Press.

Paley, V.G. (1991) *The Boy Who Would Be a Helicopter* (reprint ed.). Cambridge, MA: Harvard University Press.

Paley, V.G. (2005) *A Child's Work: The Importance of Fantasy Play.* Chicago: University of Chicago Press.

Palmer, S. (2016) *Literacy, Learning...and Luck.* Isleornay: Upstart. Accessed on 7/7/2020 at https://www.upstart.scot/literacy-learning-and-luck.

Palmer, S. (n.d.) *Expert Advisors*. Winchester: Empathy Lab. Accessed on 7/7/2020 at www.empathylab.uk/supporters1.

Panc, I., Georgescu, A. and Zaharia, M. (2015) 'Why children should learn to tell stories in primary school?' *Procedia – Social and Behavioral Sciences 187*, 591–595.

Pintrich, P.R. and Schunk, D.H. (2002) *Motivation in Education: Theory, Research, and Applications* (2nd ed.) Englewood Cliffs, NJ: Prentice Hall.

Popova, M. (2015) *Hope, Cynicism, and the Stories We Tell Ourselves*. New York: Brain Pickings. Accessed on 7/7/2020 at www.brainpickings.org/2015/02/09/hope-cynicism.

Popova, M. and Bedrick, C. (2018) *A Velocity of Being: Letters to a Young Reader*. New York: Enchanted Lion Books.

Price, L.H., Van Kleeck, A. and Huberty, C.J. (2009) 'Talk during book sharing between parents and preschool children: A comparison between storybook and expository book conditions.' *Reading Research Quarterly 44*, 2, Apr–Jun, 171–194.

Reggio Emilia Australia Information Exchange (2018) *The Hundred Languages of Children*. Hawthorn: Reggio Emilia Australia Information Exchange. Accessed on 7/7/2020 at https://reggioaustralia.org.au/the-hundred-languages-of-children.

Resnick, M. (2019) 'Projects, Passion, Peers and Play.' In R. Gawn (ed.) *Creating Creators: How Can We Enhance Creativity in Education Systems?* Billund: Lego Foundation. Accessed on 7/7/2020 at www.legofoundation.com/media/1664/creating-creators_full-report.pdf.

Rinaldi, C. (2006) *In Dialogue with Reggio Emilia: Listening, Researching and Learning*. London: Routledge.

Robinson, K. (2010) *Bring on the Learning Revolution*. Accessed on 7/7/2020 at http://sirkenrobinson.com/bring-on-the-learning-revolution.

Robinson, K. and Aronica, L. (2015) *Creative Schools: Revolutionizing Education from the Ground Up*. London: Penguin.

Rogoff, B., Baker-Sennett, J., Lacasa, P. and Goldsmith, D. (1995) 'Development through Participation in Sociocultural Activity.' In J.J. Goodnow, P.J. Miller and F. Kessel (eds) *New Directions for Child Development, No. 67: Cultural Practices as Contexts for Development*. San Francisco: Jossey-Bass.

Rose, F. (2011) *The Art of Immersion: How the Digital Generation Is Remaking Hollywood, Madison Avenue, and the Way We Tell Stories*. New York: W.W. Norton.

Rosen, M. (2010) 'Foreword.' In C. Tims (ed.) *Born Creative*. London: Demos. Accessed on 7/7/2020 at https://dera.ioe.ac.uk/23207/1/Born_Creative_-_web_-_final.pdf.

Rosen, M. (2017) *Why Writing Matters*. London: Michael Rosen. Accessed on 7/7/2020 at http://michaelrosenblog.blogspot.com/2017/06/why-writing-matters.html.

Russ, S.W. (2004) *Play in Child Development and Psychotherapy*. Mahwah, NJ: Erlbaum.

Russo, J. and Russo, T. (2017) 'Using Rich Narratives to Engage Students in Mathematics: A Narrative-First Approach.' In R. Seah, M. Horne, J. Ocean and C. Orellana (eds) *Proceedings of the 54th Conference of the Mathematics Association of Victoria*. Melbourne: Mathematics Association of Victoria.

Sacks, O. (1998) *The Man Who Mistook His Wife for a Hat*. New York: Touchstone Books

Sartre, J.P. (1964) *Nausea*. New York: New Directions.

Schank, R.C. (2002) 'Every curriculum tells a story.' *International Journal of Cognition and Technology 1*, 1, 169–182.

Schiappa, E., Gregg, P.B. and Hewes, D.E. (2005) 'The parasocial contact hypothesis.' *Communication Monographs 72*, 92–115.

Schleicher, A. (2019) 'Assessing Creative Learning to Empower Learners in Creating Creators.' In R. Gawn (ed.) *Creating Creators: How Can We Enhance Creativity in Education Systems?* Billund: Lego Foundation. Accessed on 7/7/2020 at www.legofoundation.com/media/1664/creating-creators_full-report.pdf.

Schwartz, K. (2013) *How Visual Thinking Improves Writing.* San Francisco: KQED. Accessed on 7/7/2020 at www.kqed.org/mindshift/32318/how-visual-thinking-improves-writing.

Seden, J. (2008) 'Creative connections: Parenting capacity, reading with children and practitioner assessment and intervention.' *Child and Family Social Work 13*, 133–143.

Seja, A.L. and Russ, S.W. (1999) 'Children's fantasy play and emotional understanding.' *Journal of Clinical Child Psychology 28*, 269–277.

Senehi, J. (2002) 'Constructive storytelling: A peace process.' *Peace and Conflict Studies 9*, 2, art. 3. Accessed on 7/7/2020 at http://nsuworks.nova.edu/pcs/vol9/iss2/3.

Serafini, F. (2014) 'Exploring wordless picture books.' *The Reading Teacher 68*, 1, 24–26.

Serrouk, F. (2017) 'Young Children Need Stories in Which They Can Recognise Their Own Lives.' London: Maze Media. Accessed on 7/7/2020 at www.teachwire.net/news/young-children-need-stories-in-which-they-can-recognise-their-own-lives-and?utm_content=bufferfe894&utm_medium=social&utm_source=twitter.com&utm_campaign=buffer.

Singer, D.G. and Singer, J.L. (1990) 'The house of make believe: Children's play and the developing imagination.' Cambridge, MA: Harvard University Press.

Singer, D.G. and Singer, J.L. (2005) *Imagination and Play in the Electronic Age.* Cambridge, MA: Harvard University Press.

Singer, J.L. and Lythcott, M.A. (2004) 'Fostering School Achievement and Creativity through Sociodramatic Play in the Classroom.' In E.F. Zigler, D.G. Singer and S.J. Bishop-Joseph (eds) *Children's Play: The Roots of Reading.* Washington, DC: Zero to Three Press.

Sipe, L.R. (2000) '"Those two gingerbread boys could be brothers": How children use intertextual connections during storybook read-alouds.' *Children's Literature in Education 31*, 2, 73–90.

Sisk-Hilton, S. and Meier, D.R. (2017) *Narrative Inquiry in Early Childhood and Elementary School: Learning to Teach, Teaching Well.* New York: Routledge.

Slade, S. and Wolf, D.P. (1999) *Play: Clinical and Developmental Approaches to Meaning and Representation.* Oxford: Oxford University Press.

Smith, P.K., Cowie, H. and Blades, M. (2003) *Understanding Children's Development* (4th ed). Oxford: Blackwell.

Souter-Anderson, L. (2010) *Touching Clay: Touching What? The Use of Clay in Therapy.* Blandford: Archive Publishing.

South Africa Book Development Council (2007) *National Survey into the Reading and Book Reading Behaviour of Adult South Africans: Quantitative Research into the Reading and Book Buying Habits of Adult South Africans from Age 16.* Pretoria: Print Industries Council, Dept. of Arts and Culture.

Stadler, M.A. and Ward, G.C. (2005) 'Supporting the narrative development of young children.' *Early Childhood Education Journal 33*, 2, 73–80.

Steering Committee for the Review of Government Service Provision (2011) *Report on Government Services: Indigenous Compendium.* Productivity Commission, Canberra.

Stephens, G.J., Silbert, L.J. and Hasson, U. (2010) 'Speaker-listener neural coupling underlies successful communication.' *Proceedings of the National Academy of Sciences 107*, 32, 14425–14430.

Stites, L.J. and Özçalışkan, Ş. (2017) 'Who did what to whom? Children track story referents first in gesture.' *Journal of Psycholinguistic Research 46*, 4, 1019–1032.

Storr, W. (2019) *The Science of Storytelling*. London: William Collins.

Storrs, C. (2016) *This Is Your Child's Brain on Reading*. Atlanta: CNN. Accessed on 7/7/2020 at https://edition.cnn.com/2015/08/05/health/parents-reading-to-kids-study/index.html.

Stott, F. and Bowman, B. (1996) 'Child development knowledge: A slippery base for practice.' *Early Childhood Research Quarterly 11*, 169–183.

Sullivan, A. and Strang, H. (2002/2003) 'Bibliotherapy in the classroom.' *Childhood Education 79*, 2, 74–80.

Sunderland, M. (2000) *Using Story Telling as a Therapeutic Tool with Children*. Bicester: Speechmark Publishing.

Susperreguy, M.I. and Davis-Kean, P.E. (2016) 'Maternal math talk in the home and math skills in preschool children.' *Early Education and Development 27*, 6, 841–857.

Sydik, J.J. (2016) 'Hey, Where's the Monster? How a Storytelling Game Is Played in a Preschool Classroom.' Doctoral thesis, College of Education and Human Sciences, Lincoln. Accessed on 7/7/2020 at https://digitalcommons.unl.edu/cgi/viewcontent.cgi?article=1282&context=cehsdiss.

Thompson, R.A. (2009) 'Doing what doesn't come naturally: The development of self-regulation.' *Zero to Three Journal 30*, 2, 33–39.

Turner, C. and Kamenetz, A. (2019) *The Key to Raising Brilliant Kids? Play A Game*. Washington, DC: NPR. Accessed on 6/7/2020 at www.npr.org/2019/10/10/769052767/the-key-to-raising-brilliant-kids-play-a-game?t=1586271679050&t=1588249887131.

UK Parliament (2017) *'High-Stakes' Testing Harming Teaching and Learning in Primary Schools*. London: UK Parliament. Accessed on 7/7/2020 at www.parliament.uk/business/committees/committees-a-z/commons-select/education-committee/news-parliament-2015/primary-assessment-report-published-16-17.

United Nations Educational Scientific and Cultural Organization (UNESCO) (2006) *Education for All: Literacy for Life*. EFA Global Monitoring Report. Paris: UNESCO Publishing.

University of Nevada (2010) *Books in the Home as Important as Parents' Education Level*. Reno: University of Nevada. Accessed on 7/7/2020 at www.unr.edu/nevada-today/news/2010/books-in-the-home-as-important-as-parents-education-level.

Valentini, A., Ricketts, J., Pye, R.E. and Houston-Price, C. (2018) 'Listening while reading promotes word learning from stories.' *Journal of Experimental Child Psychology 167*, 10–31.

van der Kolk, B. (2015a) *Trauma in the Body: Interview with Dr. Bessel van der Kolk*. Foxborough: Still Harbor. Accessed on 7/7/2020 at www.stillharbor.org/anchormagazine/2015/11/18/trauma-in-the-body.

van der Kolk, B. (2015b) *The Body Keeps the Score: Mind, Brain and Body in the Transformation of Trauma*. New York: Penguin Random House.

Vezzali, L., Stathi, S., Giovannini, D., Capozza, D. and Trifiletti, E. (2015) 'The greatest magic of Harry Potter: Reducing prejudice.' *Journal of Applied Social Psychology 45*, 2, 105–121.

Vlaicu, C. and Voicu, C. (2013) 'Supporting adolescent identity development through personal narratives.' *Procedia – Social and Behavioral Sciences 92*, 1026–1032.

Walker, S., Wachs, T., Gardner, J., Lozoff, B. *et al.* (2007) 'Child development: Risk factors for adverse outcomes in developing countries.' *The Lancet 369*, 145–157.

Walsh, I., Scullion, M., Burns, S., MacEvilly, D. and Brosnan, G. (2011) 'Social not solo: Narrative telling and children with AD(H)D.' American Speech & Hearing Association (ASHA) Annual Convention, San Diego.

Walton, A. and Hinrichsen, N. (2006) *A Very Nice Day*. Cape Town: Tafelberg Publishers.

Ward, E. (2010) 'New Spaces for Watchful Creatures: Family Learning at the Whitworth Art Gallery.' In C. Tims (ed.) *Born Creative*. London: Demos. Accessed on 7/7/2020 at https://dera.ioe.ac.uk/23207/1/Born_Creative_-_web_-_final.pdf.

Weigel, D.J., Martin, S.S. and Bennett, K.K. (2010) 'Pathways to literacy: Connections between family assets and preschool children's emergent literacy skills.' *Journal of Early Childhood Research 8*, 1, 5–22.

Wells, G. (1986) *The Meaning Makers: Children Learning Language and Using Language to Learn*. Portsmouth, NH: Heinemann.

Wells, G. (1999) *Dialogic Inquiry: Towards a Sociocultural Practice and Theory of Education*. New York: Cambridge University Press.

Wertsch, J.V. and Tulviste, P. (1996) 'L.S. Vygotsky and Contemporary Developmental Psychology.' In H. Daniels (ed.) *An Introduction to Vygotsky*. London: Routledge.

White, R., Prager, E., Schaefer, C., Kross, E., Duckworth, A. and Carlson, S. (2016) 'The "Batman effect": Improving perseverance in young children.' *Child Development 88*, 5

Widen, S.C., Pochedly, J.T. and Russell, J.A. (2015) 'The development of emotion concepts: A story superiority effect in older children and adolescents.' *Journal of Experimental Child Psychology 131*, 186–192.

Wielenga, C. (2013) 'Shattered stories: Healing and reconciliation in the South African context.' *Verbum et Ecclesia 34*, 1, art. 747.

Wigmore, T. (2016) 'Why English Schoolchildren Are So Unhappy.' London: New Statesman. Accessed on 7/7/2020 at www.newstatesman.com/politics/education/2016/05/why-english-schoolchildren-are-so-unhappy.

Williams, B.O. (1994) 'Wordless books: Every picture tells a story: The magic of wordless books.' *School Library Journal 41*, 8, 38–40.

Winick, S. (2013) *Einstein's Folklore*. Washington, DC: Library of Congress. Accessed on 7/7/2020 at https://blogs.loc.gov/folklife/2013/12/einsteins-folklore/.

Woolcock, N. (2016) 'I was used as window dressing, says sacked mental health champion.' The Times. Accessed on 16/11/2020 at https://www.thetimes.co.uk/article/i-was-used-as-window-dressing-says-sacked-mental-health-champion-tcmj7j8j3.

Wunungmurra, W. (1989) 'Dhawurrpunaramirr: Finding the common ground for a new Aboriginal curriculum.' *Ngoonjook: A Journal of Australian Indigenous Issues 2*, 7–19.

York University (2017) *Children Show Implicit Racial Bias from a Young Age, Research Finds: New Research Sheds Light on How Racial Prejudice Develops*. Rockville: ScienceDaily. Accessed on 7/7/2020 at www.sciencedaily.com/releases/2017/11/171127152100.htm.

Zak, P.J. (2013) *How Stories Change the Brain*. Berkeley: Greater Good Science Center. Accessed on 7/7/2020 at https://greatergood.berkeley.edu/article/item/how_stories_change_brain.

Zak, P.J. (2014) 'Why Your Brain Loves Good Storytelling.' Boston: Harvard Business Review. Accessed on 7/7/2020 at https://hbr.org/2014/10/why-your-brain-loves-good-storytelling.

Zak, P.J. (2015) 'Why inspiring stories make us react: The neuroscience of narrative.' *Cerebrum*, art. 2.

Zipes, J. (2013) *The Irresistible Fairy Tale: The Cultural and Social History of a Genre*. Princeton: Princeton University Press.

Index

Sub-headings in *italics* indicate tables and figures.